Key Concepts in Adult Education and Training

As adults, we are all continually involved in learning, with increasing numbers of us engaged in more formalized forms of learning; that is, in education or training. All those involved in the broad field of adult education and training will come into contact with many specialist ideas or concepts. It is often assumed of students that they already have a general understanding of these concepts, their meanings, applicability and interrelationships. This is not always the case.

This book examines in detail over forty of these key concepts, ranging from community education and experiential learning to competence and access. It presents a clear, analytical discussion in jargon-free language. It is, therefore, indispensable to all students and practitioners of adult education and training.

Malcolm Tight is a Reader in Continuing Education at the University of Warwick. He previously worked at Birkbeck College and the Open University. He researches post-compulsory education policy and practice, and the relations between adult and organizational learning.

Key Concepts in Adult Education and Training

Malcolm Tight

London and New York

First published 1996
by Routledge
11 New Fetter Lane, London EC4P 4EE

Simultaneously published in the USA and Canada
by Routledge
29 West 35th Street, New York, NY 10001

Routledge is an International Thomson Publishing Company

© 1996 Malcolm Tight

Typeset in Palatino by
Florencetype Ltd, Stoodleigh, Devon

Printed and bound in Great Britain by
Clays Ltd, St Ives PLC

British Library Cataloguing in Publication Data
A catalogue record for this book is available from the
British Library

Library of Congress Cataloguing in Publication Data
Tight, Malcolm.
  Key concepts in adult education and training /
by Malcolm Tight.
  Includes bibliographical references and index.
    1. Adult education.   2. Adult education – study and
teaching.   I. Title.
LC5215.T57 1996   95–25982
374'.1 – dc20   CIP

ISBN 0–415–12833–1 (hbk)
ISBN 0–415–12834–X (pbk)

For Christina,
with all my love

Contents

Figures

Introduction

CONCEPTS IN ADULT EDUCATION AND TRAINING

Adult education and training is an important and developing field of activity and study. As children and as adults, we are all engaged in learning every day of our lives, whether we realize it or not. We are also increasingly likely to be involved in more formalized forms of learning – that is, in education or training – both immediately after we have completed the compulsory education period and throughout the rest of our lives. In the UK, for example, participation surveys (see the section on participation in Chapter 7) indicate that every year at least one in five adults are involved in education or training.

Many thousands of us are currently employed to assist and guide the learning of other adults: as teachers or trainers, as lecturers or facilitators, as advisors or managers. We may be employed as such full time or part time, or this role may form only one part of a more general portfolio of supervisory responsibilities. We may work in a designated institution of education or training. We may work for other public, private or voluntary sector organizations, which have a concern for the development of their employees or workers. Or we may work on our own account.

Every year, large numbers of those involved in the education and training of adults themselves undertake some form of education or training to support or prepare them for these roles. This professional development may take place at a variety of levels: for City & Guilds qualifications, for the Certificate in Education (Further Education), for first degrees, for the qualifications of professional bodies (e.g. the Institute of Personnel Development), for Masters courses, or for research degrees. Or it may not involve any qualification at all, and may indeed be entirely self-directed.

All who study or research adult education and training, or are involved in its delivery, will come into contact with many ideas or concepts which are of importance to the field. If they are studying for a relevant qualification, they will probably have to write essays or assignments about them. More commonly, they will be expected to have a general understanding of their meaning, applicability and interrelationships.

This book is designed for people in these positions, who have some responsibility for, and/or interest in, adult education and training, and who wish to develop their understanding of the many associated concepts. Written in an accessible, and relatively jargon-free style, the book contains plentiful references for those who would like to investigate particular concepts in more detail.

The book aims to offer a map of the field and a framework for further study. It certainly does not seek to provide the last word: whole books could be written about any of the concepts discussed here, and, as the references indicate, they have been. Nor does it offer the kind of conceptual analysis practised by philosophers or linguists for other philosophers or linguists. The style of writing, while critical and demanding, is intended both to demystify and encourage interest on a broader front.

A CONTESTED TERRAIN

What, then, are concepts? In essence, they are words that label ideas which are of key importance to us. Examples from general conversation would include truth, beauty, evil, time, hunger, love and destiny. Concepts have, therefore, a resonance which goes beyond that of more ordinary words. This resonance depends crucially, of course, upon the context. Thus, words which are key concepts for adult educators and trainers may just be ordinary words for others, and vice versa. The same is true within the field of adult education and training, so that different practitioners or participants will emphasize different concepts.

From this brief account, it will be apparent that particular concepts may not have the same meaning or meanings for all. Indeed, it is a characteristic of concepts that their interpretation and usage varies: in other words, they are contested. They may be accorded varied meanings by different interest groups; including individual educators or trainers, representative bodies, employers and trades unions, central and local government, and international organizations. These understandings will also vary across time and space.

Historically, concepts may come and go as policy imperatives and fashions change. Some will retain their underlying importance, though their interpretation and coverage may change. Some may be reinvented from time to time, but given new labels. In spatial terms, the meaning and significance of concepts may vary from country to country, region to region, even from town to town. Thus, it is common to find different terms used – or the same terms used differently – in, for example, industrialized and developing nations, and in anglophone and francophone countries.

At this point, it has to be recognized that the terms used to label this book, 'adult', 'education' and 'training', are themselves contested concepts (and they will be considered as such in Chapter 1). The field of adult education and training remains broad, fractured and amorphous, differently understood, labelled and defined in different countries and by different interests. This variation and contestation is apparent from the scope, and also constitutes one of the main themes, of this book. We work in a contested terrain.

QUESTIONS OF VALUES

There is also, of course, a personal dimension. This book has no pretensions to objectivity, neutrality or balance. It offers the interpretation of one middle-aged, middle-class, able-bodied, white English man, who has been working in various capacities in the field of adult education and training for the last fifteen years. The organization of the book, the selection of the concepts for discussion and the views expressed are all in essence the author's own. Many other authors are, of course, referred to, but their ideas are mediated through the author's presentation and critique.

Other writers would undoubtedly have chosen a different selection of concepts and authors, and would have stressed a different collection of points. Indeed, I would have produced a different book if I had written it at a different time. The motivation for writing this book came largely from the perceived lack of a book of this nature, which I would have found a useful resource. Its writing was a learning journey for me, as I hope it will be for many readers in their turn.

So it may be useful to say something here relating to my own preferences, biases and values, at least insofar as I am aware of them, which the reader will then find reflected throughout the book. I would identify the following as most relevant to the present context:

- I try to take a broad view of what constitutes adult education and training, and would rather go beyond borders than confine myself within them.
- I regard adult education and training essentially as a field of practice, not as a discipline. As such, I see the work of many disciplines as being relevant to it.
- I consider myself a generalist rather than a specialist or an expert.
- I am at least as much interested in the relations between concepts as in their distinctive characteristics.
- I like to eschew jargon wherever possible (though concepts are, of course, at one level, jargon) and present the discussion in ways which should be widely intelligible.
- As already stated, I am a middle-aged, middle-class, able-bodied, white English man. As such, while I may try to take account of the perspectives of others of different age, class, ability, ethnicity, nationality and gender, I have not experienced these perspectives.
- All of the books and articles referred to in this book are written in the English language, or have been translated into English.
- The majority of the material discussed originates, therefore, from the UK or North America.
- Finally, recognizing these preferences, limitations and reservations, I have, nevertheless, endeavoured to produce a book which is as generally useful as possible.

With this brief venture into the first person completed, I will now slip back into the third person, with which, as an academic, I am naturally rather happier.

Core concepts	adult, education, training, learning, teaching, development, vocational or liberal?
International concepts	lifelong, recurrent, the learning organization, the learning society
Institutional concepts	further and higher, adult and continuing, community, formal, non-formal, informal
Work-related concepts	human capital, human resource development, career, professional
Learning concepts	distance, open, flexible, experiential, independent, self-directed, andragogy, conscientization
Curricular concepts	knowledge and skill, capability and enterprise, competence, quality
Structural concepts	access and participation, accreditation and modularization, success and dropout

Figure I.1 The organization of the book

ORGANIZATION OF THE BOOK

This book came together through a combination of top-down and bottom-up strategies. In other words, while there was a clear plan at the beginning, there were significant changes made during its production, in terms of both overall structure and of what was, and was not, included. This occurred despite the fact that the book was essentially written in a relatively short, three-month period. Indeed, as already suggested, the writing was an illuminating and fruitful learning experience for the author.

The organization of the book is summarized in Figure I.1. From this, as from the Contents, it can be seen that the forty-odd concepts discussed have been grouped into seven chapters. While this organization was both carefully considered and, to some extent, original, the concepts might well have been grouped and labelled differently. Similarly, other concepts could have been discussed – indeed, many are referred to in passing in the body of the text – and some of those which have been discussed could have been left out.

With one exception, there is no particular significance in the ordering of the chapters. What have been referred to as the core concepts (see the next section) are discussed first: the remaining chapters could have been placed in almost any order. As the reader will note, many cross-references have been made between the chapters in an attempt to elucidate the relationships between the concepts discussed.

It would, of course, have been possible to have organized the book in a dictionary or encyclopedia format, with the concepts discussed in alphabetical order. They have, however, been linked together in groups of some coherence, so as to allow a more comparative, linked and flowing discussion. The labels used to identify the groups and chapters – core, international, institutional, work-related, learning, curricular, structural – are not, however, put forward as in any way definitive. They are my own conceptualization and basically a suggestive convenience.

CORE AND QUALIFYING CONCEPTS

Chapter 1 focuses on what have been termed the *core* concepts. In other words, these are the concepts which are the most common and central, and, therefore, the most essential to an understanding of the field. They include the three concepts included in the title of the book – adult, education, training – plus the related ideas of learning, teaching and development.

Chapter 2, 3, 4, 5, 6 and 7 then examine what, by contrast, may be termed *qualifying* concepts. These concepts refer to approaches to, or details of, the field as defined by the core concepts. Indeed, it is commonly the case in practice that concepts are presented as two words – one qualifying, one core – as in the cases of, for example, lifelong learning, higher

Lifelong Recurrent	
Further Higher	
Adult Continuing	
Community	
Formal Informal Non-formal	
Human resource	**Education**
Career	**Training**
Professional	**Learning**
Distance Open Flexible	**Teaching** **Development**
Experiential Independent Self-directed	
Knowledge Skill	
Capability Enterprise	
Competence	
Quality	

Figure I.2 Core and qualifying concepts

education, skill development, distance teaching or professional training. This relationship is illustrated in Figure I.2.

In Figure I.2, the words to the right of the vertical line are the core concepts, while those to the left are the qualifying concepts. The bulk of the concepts discussed in detail in Chapters 2 to 7 have been listed on the lefthand side. In the great majority of cases, further concepts can be created by combining any of the words on the left with any of those on the right. Most of these combinations have an existing usage; even where they do not, they usually still make sense.

The major exception to this relationship appears to be the group of terms discussed in Chapter 7 under the label of 'structural concepts': access and participation, accreditation and modularization, success and dropout. The reason for this difference seems clear. The other chapters are largely concerned with examining what are, at least in part, approaches to adult education and training: for example, recurrent, community, competence, flexible, or career education, training, learning, teaching or development. In Chapter 7, however, the focus is more on the internal organization of such approaches.

FRAMEWORKS FOR ANALYSIS

How do we, or should we, go about the analysis of concepts? Philosophers and linguists, as already mentioned, have long had their own techniques of conceptual analysis (see, for example, Flew 1956). While what is presented in this book could legitimately also be termed conceptual analysis, it is not approached from an overly philosophical point of view. Rather, the aim has been to make use of a number of alternative frameworks for analysis, drawing on a variety of disciplinary traditions.

The analytical frameworks which suggest themselves for these purposes include, where relevant:

- the history and development of the concepts discussed;
- their disciplinary origins and location (e.g. biology, economics, history, management, philosophy, politics, psychology, sociology);
- their national and international policy context, and their usage in different countries;

- their treatment of underlying social variables (e.g. gender, class, 'race', age);
- their relevance to different levels of activity (e.g. individual, organization, society);
- their linkages with, and relations to, each other.

These frameworks will be utilized in each of the chapters which follow to illustrate the background, application and wider context of the concepts discussed. The final chapter, Chapter 8, will then attempt an overall evaluation of the concepts examined, of the frameworks used to analyse them, and of what this tells us about the field of study.

HOW TO USE THIS BOOK

A little guidance on how to use this book may be of assistance to some readers. It is not envisaged that many will wish, or feel the need, to read all of the way through the book, certainly not in one go. The most probable and useful strategy for most will be to focus on those chapters which cover areas or concepts of particular interest. These can be identified through the list of contents or the index, or just by browsing through the text.

In most cases, however, readers will probably have something to gain from a study of the Introduction and of the concluding chapter. These provide a general framework for considering, and some conclusions on, the use of concepts in adult education and training.

A FEW FINAL POINTS

Three points remain to be made before this Introduction is concluded. First, it is common practice in some circles to place concepts under discussion in quotation marks: thus, 'education', 'self-directed' and so forth. This has not been adopted as standard practice in this book, but has only been used where it seemed necessary to help intelligibility. To do otherwise would have been to clutter the book with quotation marks, and possibly both confuse and irritate the reader.

Second, as the earlier discussion of core and qualifying concepts will have made apparent, this book is not simply an examination of forty-odd, free-standing concepts. It is also, at least implicitly, an analysis of the more than 150 concepts which can be made by combining the different core and qualifying concepts.

It would have been wasteful and tedious, however, to keep referring to all of these possible permutations in the text. Instead, the core concepts have been used in Chapters 2 to 7 in an almost interchangeable fashion. Thus, where, for example, non-formal education is being examined, the discussion is also meant to encompass non-formal learning, non-formal training, non-formal development and non-formal teaching, unless explicitly stated to the contrary.

Third, and finally, as the reader who has already browsed through the book will have noted, the discussion is extensively referenced. This has been done in two ways, with the aim of making the book as useful to the reader as possible. At the end of each chapter you will find a selected and annotated list of some of the most useful and accessible books or articles which cover the concepts discussed there. A much more comprehensive set of references is given at the end of the book for those who wish to explore particular discussions somewhat further.

Chapter 1

The core concepts

OPPOSITIONAL OR RELATED TERMS?

This chapter examines six basic terms. Three of them – adult, education and training – form the title of this book. The other three – learning, teaching and development – are closely related. Together, these six terms can be seen as the baseline or core concepts which define, in competing ways, the breadth and nature of our whole field of study.

The final section of the chapter looks at what has been one of the key debates over many years, that between liberal and vocational emphases on education and training. Chapters 2 to 7 then analyse a more extensive series of qualifying concepts, which are widely used in association with the core concepts to signify narrower areas of interest.

As core concepts, the six terms examined in this chapter have naturally been the most widely discussed. Such discussion is commonly organized in terms of oppositions, or of inclusion and exclusion. Thus, education and training may be seen as opposing terms, the former broad, knowledge based and general, the latter narrow, skill based and specific (see also the discussion of knowledge and skill in Chapter 6). Indeed, this kind of approach is another representation of the liberal versus vocational debate reviewed in the final section. Similarly, learning may be seen in opposition to teaching, the one receptive and perhaps passive (but see the examination of self-directed learning in Chapter 5), the other directive and organizational.

Analyses based on the idea of inclusion or exclusion quite often make use of diagrams, with the concepts discussed portrayed as circles. In such cases, training may be represented

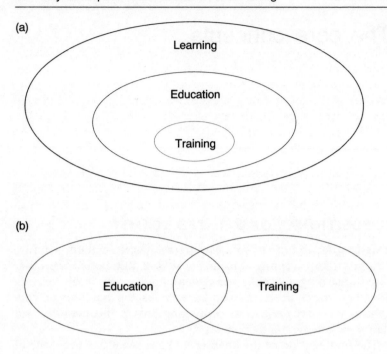

Figure 1.1 Alternative diagrammatic representations of core conceptual relations

as a small circle wholly contained within a larger circle labelled education, which itself is completely enclosed within an even larger circle called learning. Or, combining the idea of opposition with that of inclusion/exclusion, education and training may be shown as overlapping circles (see Figure 1.1). This presentation illustrates the idea that, while some learning activities may definitively be termed either education or training, in between there is a larger or smaller group of activities which might legitimately be called either or both.

While such presentations may be criticized as inevitably rather simplistic, nevertheless, they do demonstrate differing but widely held views or perceptions. This chapter aims to go a little deeper.

ADULT

What do we mean when we call someone an adult? What distinguishes adult education, adult training and adult learning from
education, training and learning in a more general sense? The
second of these questions has an institutional or organizational
context, and as such is discussed in detail in Chapter 3 (see the
section 'adult and continuing'). The former question will be
addressed in this section.

A wide range of concepts is involved when we use the term
'adult'. The word can refer to a *stage* in the life cycle of the
individual; he or she is first a child, then a youth, then an
adult. It can refer to *status*, an acceptance by society that the
person concerned has completed his or her novitiate and is
now incorporated fully into the community. It can refer to a
social *sub-set*: adults as distinct from children. Or it can include
a set of *ideals and values*: adulthood.

(Rogers 1986, p. 5, original emphasis)

At its simplest, therefore, adulthood may be defined purely in
terms of age. Thus, in England, people are generally assumed
to become adult at 18 years old, when they get the right to
vote. Until relatively recently, however, the voting age was
21 years, and there are many adult roles – for example, those
requiring a specialist education or training – which cannot
be entered into until this age or later. Similarly, some aspects of
adulthood may be exercised before reaching 18 years old, such
as marriage, full-time employment (including in the armed
forces) and taxation.

It is important to remember the qualification 'generally' here,
for adult status is not accorded to all at these ages. Thus, those
with severe disabilities may never achieve or be allowed full
adult status. The age of majority also varies somewhat from
country to country, or even within countries, in some cases occurring at an earlier age, in some cases later. Whereas in
industrialized countries the age of majority is legally defined, in
developing countries it may be more a case of local cultural
tradition. Maturity may be recognized in an essentially physical
or biological sense, related to the onset or ending of puberty,
and may vary in terms of age, not just for boys and girls but
for individuals as well.

Of course, it would be naive to believe that merely surviving long enough to wake up on one's eighteenth birthday, or passing through puberty, automatically changes one from being a child to being an adult. While the effects of puberty are externally recognizable, we do not (yet) wear barcodes on our sides recording our age, and other people's reactions to us depend, in any case, upon many factors other than our absolute age. These include, most notably, our sex and ethnicity, and the reaction will vary with the characteristics of the perceiver as well as our own.

Within industrialized countries, as Rogers (1986) indicates, we also commonly recognize an intermediary stage between childhood and adulthood. Then we may be called variously adolescents, youths or teenagers. So the transition from child to adult is not sudden or instantaneous.

The idea of 'adult' is not, therefore, directly connected to age, but is related to what generally happens as we grow older. That is, we achieve physical maturity, become capable of providing for ourselves, move away from our parents, have children of our own, and exercise a much greater role in the making of our own choices. This then affects not just how we see ourselves, but how others see us. In other words, we may see the difference between being and not being an adult as chiefly a status distinction.

Adulthood may thus be considered as a state of being which both accords status and rights to individuals and simultaneously confers duties or responsibilities upon them. We might then define adulthood as: 'an ethical status resting on the presumption of various moral and personal qualities' (Paterson 1979, p. 31). Having said that, however, we also have to recognize what a heterogeneous group of people adults are. It is this amorphous group which forms the customer base or audience for adult education and training.

EDUCATION

As adults, all of us have had a considerable experience of education, though this experience may be largely confined to our childhood, and may not be continuing. The nature of education may, therefore, seem to be relatively clear to us, with particular associations with educational institutions such as schools, colleges and universities.

Such a conceptualization – that is, that education is what takes place in educational institutions – is, however, not satisfactory for three main reasons. First, it is circular, defining each concept ('education', 'educational institution') wholly in terms of the other. Second, it tells us nothing about the qualities of education other than its location (e.g. we might just as well define oranges as 'things that grow on orange trees'). Third, with a little thought we would probably recognize that education also takes place in other kinds of institutions.

This final point is at the heart of the distinction between formal and non-formal education (see Chapter 3). The former is defined as taking place in explicitly educational institutions, and the latter in other institutions, the primary function of which is not education (e.g. churches, factories, health centres, prisons, military bases). It might also be pointed out that education may take place outside institutions altogether, as in the case of distance education (see the section on distance in Chapter 5), though here the association with an institution remains important.

The nature of education has been the subject of a considerable amount of analysis by philosophers of education (e.g. Barrow and White 1993; Hirst and Peters 1970; Peters 1967). Thus, Peters, in one of his more accessible works, identified three criteria for education:

(i) that 'education' implies the transmission of what is worthwhile to those who become committed to it;
(ii) that 'education' must involve knowledge and understanding and some kind of cognitive perspective, which are not inert;
(iii) that 'education' at least rules out some procedures of transmission, on the grounds that they lack wittingness and voluntariness on the part of the learner.

(Peters 1966, p. 45)

We can critically pick away at this quotation with relative ease. Who decides what is worthwhile, for example: the learner, the teacher, the institution, employers, the state? How much time must we allow to pass in order to detect commitment? How active (i.e. not inert) do we have to be to be judged as involved in an educational activity? In what sense can children – as distinct from adults, for whom we might at least assume some degree of voluntariness if they are participating in education – be said to be voluntarily engaged in education? Yet these comments confirm how useful accounts like that of Peters can be in identifying and delimiting many of the key questions we need to address in order satisfactorily to define the concept of education.

A rather simpler definition has been given by the United Nations Educational, Scientific and Cultural Organization (UNESCO). They view education as: 'organized and sustained instruction designed to communicate a combination of knowledge, skills and understanding valuable for all the activities of life' (quoted in Jarvis 1990, p. 105).

The key phrase here, which is not explicit in Peters' formulation, and which may be used to distinguish education from learning, appears to be 'organized and sustained instruction'. This implies the involvement of an educator of some kind, and possibly also of an institution, though the education might be mediated through the printed text or through a computer programme. It also suggests that education is not a speedy process, but takes a lengthy, though perhaps not continuous, period of time. Learning, by contrast, could be seen as not necessarily involving instruction, as often occurring over a shorter timeframe and in smaller chunks.

Clearly, distinctions of this kind are not always cut and dried. They allow us to conceive of 'education' and 'learning' as ends of the same spectrum, and as shading into each other (see Figure 1.2a). Consequently, there will be some examples which could be described quite legitimately either as education or learning or both. To some extent, therefore, the terms may be used interchangeably.

How, then, to distinguish education from training? The distinction may be seen as somewhat analogous to that between education and learning (though dependent upon our view of learning), in the sense of delimiting another dimension to the area of study. The commonest approach to making a distinction is to use the ideas of breadth and/or depth:

> Probably the clearest if not the only criterion of educational value ... is that the learning in question contributes to the development of knowledge and understanding, in both breadth and depth.
>
> (Dearden 1984, p. 90)

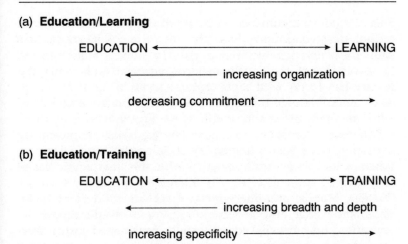

(a) **Education/Learning**

EDUCATION ◄────────────────────► LEARNING

◄──────────── increasing organization

decreasing commitment ────────────────►

(b) **Education/Training**

EDUCATION ◄────────────────────► TRAINING

◄──────────── increasing breadth and depth

increasing specificity ────────────────►

Figure 1.2 The education/learning and education/training spectra

This quotation, like the one from UNESCO, identifies education as being a general rather than a specific activity. Similarly, like both the Peters and UNESCO quotations, it portrays education as having to do with the development of knowledge and understanding. However, the UNESCO definition, unlike the other two, also specifically mentions skills development as being an educational concern. It may be argued, on the other hand, that it is understanding which is at the heart of education:

> Use of the word 'understanding', as opposed to 'knowledge', implies that what is at issue is something more than mere information and the ability to relay or act in accordance with formulae, prescriptions and instructions (the latter is characteristic of training rather than education). An ability to recite dates, answer general knowledge quizzes, or reproduce even quite complex pieces of reasoning, is not necessary to being educated. Rather one requires of an educated person that he [sic] should have internalised information, explanation, and reasoning, and made sense of it. He should understand the principles behind the specifics that he encounters; he sets particulars in a wider frame of theoretical understanding. . . . The educated person has understanding across a range of human knowledge.
>
> (Barrow and Milburn 1990, pp. 106–7)

Following these arguments, we might distinguish education from training on two grounds. First, that the former is a broader and deeper learning activity. Second, that the latter is more likely to be involved with the development of narrower skills, while the former has to do with more general levels of understanding. Once again, though, the differences are not precise and we are left with shady areas and overlaps (see Figure 1.2b).

Different approaches to understanding what is meant by education have been pursued by sociologists, focusing on its function and place within society. Within this discipline, a range of analytical approaches may be identified, including the functionalist, Marxist and interpretive (Blackledge and Hunt 1985). Thus, knowledge and understanding, the avowed purposes of education, may be viewed as socially constructed rather than absolute. The educational system may be seen as an apparatus of the state, with its function being the production of people (workers) with desired skills and qualities.

From this perspective, state education is, therefore, in the business of reproducing existing social and economic divisions (see, for example, Bourdieu and Passeron 1990; Bowles and Gintis 1976; Young 1971). Hence lies the interest of many sociologists in liberationary forms of education organized outside of the influence of the state.

From such a perspective, the meaning of education cannot, of course, be properly understood in individualistic or psychological terms, but requires an appreciation of its broader social context. This context includes not just the educational and other institutions, and other settings, within which education takes place, but a consideration of their position, relationships and linkages within society. Education thus has political, economic, technological and social ramifications. As such, it is necessarily a highly contested concept, as a brief reflection on public discussions about the topic will confirm.

TRAINING

The idea of training is most usually associated with preparing someone for performing a task or role, typically, but not necessarily, in a work setting (e.g. Buckley and Caple 1990; Nadler and Nadler 1990; Jarvis 1990). As such, it forms part of the broader fields of development (considered later in this chapter) and human resource development (a concept discussed in Chapter 4). It may also be seen, however, as a specific element or outcome of a more general process of education. Peters again offers one definition:

> The concept of 'training' has application when (i) there is some specifiable type of performance that has to be mastered, (ii) practice is required for the mastery of it, (iii) little emphasis is placed on the underlying *rationale*.
>
> (Peters 1967, p. 15, original emphasis)

This definition stresses the idea of 'mastering' the task or role, and the need for repetitive practice to enable the individual to do so, while suggesting that the actual performance might be fairly mechanical and uninformed by any underlying knowledge or understanding.

Other definitions also concern themselves with the location of the training to be undertaken:

> Training is defined as the systematic acquisition of skills, rules, concepts or attitudes that result in improved performance in the work situation. In some of these instances, such as direct on-the-job training, the instructional environment is very similar if not identical to the on-the-job environment. In other instances, the training occurs in a place far removed from the actual worksite, such as a classroom.
>
> (Goldstein and Gessner 1988, p. 43)

Interestingly, this definition extends the function of training beyond the previous one, making it clear that training may be related to behaviours at least as much as to tasks. We might question here whether, if the trainer is seeking to instil concepts and attitudes, this can be done effectively without developing the trainee's underlying knowledge and understanding. While broadening its function, this second definition narrows the location of training, by focusing on work-related training, whether this is actually work based or not.

A third definition makes clearer the potentially wide scope of the term:

> Training typically involves instruction and practice aimed at reaching a particular level of competence or operative efficiency. As a result of training we are able to respond

adequately and appropriately to some expected and typical situation. Often training addresses itself to improving performance in direct dealing with things. Thus it is necessary to train drivers and pilots, carpenters and surgeons, electricians and computer programmers. Other sorts of training are more concerned with dealing with people, as with training in sales techniques, training for supervisory positions or assertiveness training for women. Yet other kinds of training are more indirectly concerned with changing or controlling people or things, such as training to be an architect, lawyer or administrator.

(Dearden 1984, p. 59)

Dearden uses the idea of competence rather than performance (see the section on competence in Chapter 6). He limits the concept to preparing people to respond to common situations, while demonstrating its application to jobs of greater or lesser status. He also brings in a useful threefold typology of training to distinguish between dealing with things, with people, and with change or control. The third category includes examples which might equally be thought of as education, illustrating the overlap which may be recognized between these two key terms.

Ideas about training, as well as its practice, are, as in many other areas, subject to fashion and development. It is quite common to recognize four waves of change in training and development practice since the Second World War. The first wave focused on job skills training; the second, from the 1970s onwards, on management and supervisory training; and the third, in the 1980s, on organizational development and performance technology. We are now, supposedly, dealing with the fourth wave, the focus of which is on information, knowledge and wisdom (Romiszowski 1990; Toffler 1980). Once again, the last of these suggests a close linkage with education.

While practitioners and academics may have fairly clear, if varied, ideas about the meaning of training, these are not necessarily shared by people in general. For, though most people probably have a reasonably common understanding of the term 'education', associating it with schools, colleges, universities and other educational institutions, the same cannot be said of their views of training. A recent British study of this issue came to the following conclusions:

- that the general population uses the term *training* to refer to a much narrower set of activities than those understood by training professionals
- that for most people training is that which happens in formal courses
- that employers have a narrower definition of training than employees
- that activities included in the definition of training will vary across subgroups of the population
- that activities which are self-initiated and/or self-funded are less likely to be included
- that for most people training is vocationally linked
- that there is a fuzzy boundary between training and education for most people.

(Campanelli *et al.* 1994, p. 92)

The sponsors of the study in question, the Department of Employment, may well have cause to be concerned by these findings. It might well be the case that such a lack of shared conceptual clarity may be one factor limiting the development of the British vocational education and training system.

LEARNING

Learning, like breathing, is something everyone does all of the time – 'you are never too old to learn' – even if they do not realize that they are doing it. It is a fundamental human process. Unlike breathing (and unlike, as argued above, education), however, there is no common understanding of how we learn, and there are many and divergent opinions amongst psychologists and educators about just what learning is:

> The older and more traditional view of learning (the one held by Francis Bacon in 1674, for example), and the one prevalent in almost all education theory as well as in some psychological writings ... sees learning in terms of its objectives or outcomes.... To most classical learning theorists (for example, Pavlov, Thorndike and Skinner), however, as well as to more contemporary contributors such as Mezirow, Lovell and Schon, learning is basically a verb.

(Thomas 1991, p. 3)

There is not space, and it would not be appropriate, to review the full range of behavioural, cognitive and humanistic learning theories here (for such a review, see, for example, Cross 1981; Curzon 1990; Tennant 1988). The difference between those who regard learning as an outcome and those who see it as a process may be readily demonstrated, however, by comparing the views of two of the most prominent recent learning theorists, Gagné and Kolb.

Gagné develops a systems approach to learning and offers an information processing model. He identifies the elements of the learning event as consisting of the learner, a stimulus situation, the learner's memory and their response to the stimulus. What is learned may consist of intellectual skills, verbal information, cognitive strategies, motor skills or attitudes. Different types of learning are recognized at successively higher hierarchical levels: signal learning, stimulus-response learning, motor and verbal chaining, multiple discrimination, concept learning, rule learning, problem solving. For Gagné, 'Learning is a change in human disposition or capability that persists over a period of time and is not simply ascribable to processes of growth' (Gagné 1985, p. 2).

Kolb, on the other hand, builds on the work of Lewin, Dewey and Piaget. He argues that learning is best conceived as a process, not in terms of outcomes; that it is a continuous process grounded in experience; that this process requires the resolution of conflicts between different ways of looking at the world; that learning is an holistic process of adaptation to the world; that it involves transactions between the learner and the environment; and that it is the process of creating knowledge. In short: 'Learning is the process whereby knowledge is created through the transformation of experience' (Kolb 1984, p. 38). Kolb's approach has arguably been the more influential in recent years in adult education and training circles, and may be seen to underlie much of contemporary 'learning to learn' practice (see, for example, Smith 1983).

Kolb's work has also been a major stimulus for the development of experiential learning as a concept and method (see the discussion of experiential in Chapter 5). Thus, for example, some researchers have stressed the idea of critical reflection within Kolb's theory, emphasizing the importance of this part of the process if the greatest benefit is to be derived from the learning experience (Boud *et al.* 1985). Others have conceptualized critical reflection as a 'learning conversation': 'a form of dialogue about a learning experience in which the learner reflects on some event or activity in the past' (Candy, *et al.* 1985, p. 102). Such reflection might take place with the assistance of a teacher or facilitator, though with practice it might be carried out by the learner alone.

We may, however, recognize other views of learning than that it is an outcome or a process. Jarvis gives five meanings for the concept:

> 1. Any more or less permanent change in behaviour as a result of experience. 2. A relatively permanent change in behaviour which occurs as a result of practice. 3. The process whereby knowledge is created through the transformation of experience. 4. The processes of transforming experience into knowledge, skills and attitudes. 5. Memorizing information.
>
> (Jarvis 1990, p. 196)

The first two of these definitions may be related to Gagné's, but distinguish between behaviour change occurring as a result of experience or of practice (the latter suggesting a more deliberate, educational or training, event). The change in behaviour is required to be more than temporary if it is to constitute learning, so as to differentiate the event from chance occurrences and changes due to the maturation of the individual concerned.

The third and fourth of the meanings identified by Jarvis are closer to Kolb's views, with the former being an almost direct quotation from his writings. The latter definition adds skills and attitudes to knowledge as possible learning outcomes (see the section on knowledge and skill in Chapter 6). These additions make learning as explicitly relevant to training as it is to education.

The final meaning given by Jarvis for learning is what might be called a more commonplace view. The two words, 'memorizing information', take the author (and probably many of his readers) straight back to schooldays. There is a *frisson* of terror surrounding the images which these words invoke; of a child (one's former self) desperately trying to commit more and more facts to memory in order to pass an examination. This is a long way from behaviour change, or from critically reflecting on our learning experiences and having internalized conversations about them.

From the practitioner's point of view, there are at least three major deficiencies in most of these views of, and theories about, learning. One is the lack of consensus already referred to, so that there is no definitive guidance on the most effective way or ways of encouraging worthwhile learning. In practice, of course, it might be expected that learning and teaching methods would be varied, as appropriate, to take account of the individuals involved, the learning tasks and the circumstances in which the learning was taking place.

A second deficiency is the focus of most researchers upon the individual learner. We have to recognize, particularly when we are dealing with adults, that all learning takes place within a social context (Jarvis 1987), and involves the learner interacting with others individually, in groups, within organizations and in communities.

The third problem has to do with the distance which theorizing often moves us away from the subject of the theorizing; in this case, learners and how they learn. The recognition of this problem is part of the reason for the development of alternative approaches to learning theory. These may be based more directly upon what students' say they do when studying (e.g. Entwistle and Ramsden 1983; Marton, Hounsell and Entwistle 1984; Richardson *et al.* 1987), or on the identification of alternative 'learning styles' (Honey and Mumford 1986).

For the educator, teacher, facilitator or trainer, as well as for the learner, the business of adult learning comes down to a largely rule-of-thumb or heuristic approach. In other words, if it works, do it again; if it doesn't, modify it or try another approach altogether. Hence, most textbooks for adult educators and trainers, while they give due attention to learning theory, resort to a 'cookbook' type approach when it comes to giving practical advice (see, for example, Brookfield 1986; Buckley and Caple 1990; Rogers 1989; Tennant 1988).

TEACHING

The idea of teaching may be thought of as a natural complement to those of learning and education. In the case of training, however, a different complementary term would probably be used, such as trainer or facilitator. These concepts fit together in pair bonds as tight as those of Romeo and Juliet, or Cain and

Abel. In order to learn, the reasoning runs, you have to be taught. However, as has already been suggested, learning may take place without the direct presence of a teacher, so the relationship is really the other way round; in order to teach, you need at least one learner: 'Teaching is a practical activity in which a "learned" person (to use an archaism) "learns" his [sic] pupils' (Oakeshott 1967, p. 157).

As can be discerned from the use of the terms 'teacher' and 'pupil' in both this and the following quotation, teaching is usually thought of as taking place in a school or classroom setting:

> A teaching activity is the activity of a person, A (the teacher), the intention of which is to bring about an activity (learning) by a person, B (the pupil), the intention of which is to achieve some end-state (e.g. knowing, appreciating) whose object is X (e.g. a belief, attitude, skill).
>
> (Hirst 1974, p. 108)

For adult educators and trainers, and those who see learning as a lifelong process, such definitions may be regarded as unduly restricted. There has, therefore, been an understandable reaction in the field against narrow interpretations of teaching:

> It would seem that to most people, teaching involves keeping order in the class, pouring forth facts, usually through lectures or textbooks, giving examinations, and setting grades. This stereotype is badly in need of overhauling. . . . The primary task of the teacher is to *permit* the student to learn, to feed his or her curiosity.
>
> (Rogers *et al.* 1983, pp. 17–18, original emphasis)

This reaction has led many working in adult education and training to reject the term 'teacher' itself, in part from a wish to distinguish themselves from schoolteachers, and in part because of the perceived inappropriateness of what are seen as typically schoolteaching methods to adults (see also the discussion of andragogy in Chapter 5). Thus, in addition to educators or trainers, we may style ourselves facilitators, tutors, lecturers, human resource developers, change agents and many other terms.

The first of these alternatives, for example, has been defined in the following fashion:

a *facilitator* . . . is a person who has the role of helping participants to learn in an experiential group. . . . Teaching is no
longer seen as imparting and doing things to the student, but
is redefined as *facilitation of self-directed learning*.

(Heron 1989, pp. 11–12, original emphasis)

The use here of the terms 'experiential' and 'self-directed learning' makes the connections with the field of adult education
and training clearer (see the section on experiential, independent
and self-directed learning in Chapter 5). It does not, of course,
preclude the use of such approaches in the education of children.

Yet, whatever 'teachers' may call themselves, they remain
primarily concerned with how best to encourage and develop
relevant learning in their clients. As adult educators or trainers,
however, the focus of attention is less likely to be on methods
or models for teaching (Brady 1985; Joyce *et al.* 1992), and more
likely to be on learning and learning processes: 'The learning
process may . . . be defined as a series of events which lead up
to a change in behaviour and which are thought to be causally
related to the change' (Lawson 1974, p. 88).

The problem and the challenge for the 'teacher' of adults may
then be seen as revolving around the usual sub-processes of
needs identification, programme planning, delivery and evaluation. The main distinctions between adult learning and child
education can be seen to lie in the extent to which the former
involves negotiation, recognition of experience and some kind
of partnership between learner and teacher, trainer, facilitator or
whatever.

DEVELOPMENT

Development, for present purposes, may be viewed as operating
at a variety of levels: macro, meso and micro. At the macro level,
it has to do with nations and international relationships, while
at the micro level it is individual and personal. In between, at
the meso level, it has relevance for organizations and communities. All of these levels are relevant to adult education and
training, and there are connections between them.

There are a number of related concepts in widespread use
which are almost synonyms for development. Thus, the
term 'growth' is often used in a similar fashion to development,

particularly at the national and individual levels. More generally, it is also common to speak of 'change'. Perhaps most controversially, there are ideas like progress and modernization, which more clearly embody notions of direction and betterment. All of these terms implicitly or explicitly, have to do with the relationships and interdependencies between individuals, organizations or nations.

At the national level, development may be viewed wholly from an economic perspective, defined and measured in terms of output, and expressed quantitatively in terms of monetary units. It then has to do with how much is being produced by the individuals and organizations within the nation, with how efficient that production is, and how this is improving. Thus, we speak of more or less developed countries, systems or regions. Education and training are seen as contributing to national development by increasing the knowledge and skills of workers, and hence their output and productivity (see also the discussion of work-related concepts in Chapter 4).

From this economic perspective, the notions of development and growth may be distinguished:

> Although economic development is conventionally defined in terms of a rise in real gross national product (GNP) per capita, a distinction can usefully be made between development and growth. Growth may involve no major change in factor inputs nor any transformations in existing institutions. By contrast, development presupposes a process of innovation in which new technologies will be generated and new input and output mixes will emerge.
>
> (Foster 1987, p. 93)

Those involved in development studies, however, are likely to see development as an interdisciplinary concept, with cultural, political and social components in addition to the economic and technological ones (Hettne 1990). From this broader perspective:

> Development is used ... to describe the process of economic and social transformation within countries. This process often follows a well-ordered sequence and exhibits common characteristics across countries.... We can say that development has occurred when there has been an improvement in basic

needs, when economic progress has contributed to a greater sense of self-esteem for the country and the individuals within it, and when material advancement has expanded the range of choice for individuals.

(Thirlwall 1994, p. 9)

A clear linkage is made here between national and individual impacts. It is also being suggested, though this is by no means generally accepted, that nations tend to proceed along a common trajectory of development, with less developed countries repeating the history of developed countries as they pass through the process.

Of course, it is rather more complex than that. The single trajectory model for development seems unnecessarily simplistic, given the diversity of cultures across the world. Even at the most general level, different development paths may be traced for the older and newly industrialized countries: Taiwan and Singapore are not simply repeating the experience of Britain and Germany.

The relative positions of developed and developing are also in a state of constant flux, as developed countries are themselves continuing to develop. Indeed, it is the developed countries which may be seen as effectively defining the development relationship: 'The relationship of developers and those to-be-developed is constituted by the developer's knowledge and categories' (Hobart 1993, p. 2). In practice, therefore, a whole range of theories of development – positivist, radical, Marxist – may be identified (Preston 1982, 1985).

If these criticisms are accepted, it becomes inadequate to see the concept simply in terms of some idea of progress, with developing countries catching up by following the historical example of developed countries. Rather, at the macro level, development may be viewed as concerning the web of relationships, dependencies and inequalities between developed and developing countries.

When seen in personal terms, the concept has an analogous set of meanings:

Development is the all-important primary process, through which individual and organizational growth can through time achieve its fullest potential. Education is a major contributor to that developmental process, because it directly and continuously affects the formation not only of knowledge and abilities, but also of character and of culture, aspirations and achievements. Training is the shorter-term, systematic process through which an individual is helped to master defined tasks or areas of skill and knowledge to pre-determined standards.

(Harrison 1992, p. 4)

Other discussions similarly differentiate development from training (e.g. Buckley and Caple 1990). The word 'development' also appears in the term human resource development (discussed in Chapter 4), which has to do with the role of encouraging, arranging and promoting individuals' development, particularly in an organizational and employment context.

Development at the personal level need not, however, have a vocational implication or context. It may, like development at the national level, be liberal, radical or political in nature. Thus, Freire's idea of 'conscientization' (discussed in Chapter 5), formulated originally through literacy work in disadvantaged communities, may be interpreted as being primarily about individual and community development.

More generally, it is commonplace to see the roles of adult educators and trainers as being primarily concerned with the development of learners: as individuals, within groups or organizations, and within society as a whole. We may, thus, see clear linkages, in terms of development, between individual and national levels; whether these are mediated through economic or community organizations, and whether the development process emphasizes vocational, liberal or radical change.

VOCATIONAL OR LIBERAL?

The discussion in this chapter will have made clear, if it was not already apparent to the reader, some of the tensions which exist regarding the understanding of the field of adult education and training. One of the most prevalent of these tensions is that between vocational and non-vocational or liberal interpretations of education and training. This tension is apparent in the very terms 'education' and 'training', as well as within concepts such as 'development' and 'growth'.

This tension has a long history, probably going as far back as the history of the core concepts themselves, and continues to underlie a very active contemporary debate. It is also subject to the swings of fashion; so that, while the liberal view dominated European and North American discussions for much of the post-war period, the vocational view has been prominent for at least the last decade (see also Chapter 4, which discusses work-related concepts).

These changes in emphasis have affected adult education and training at least as much as, and arguably more than, child education (Crombie and Harries-Jenkins 1983; McIlroy and Spencer 1988). Thus, in Britain, older practitioners of adult education in the universities may still hark back to the 'great tradition' of the tutorial class, associated with the names of those such as Mansbridge and Tawney. In such classes, groups of earnest workers dedicated themselves to the serious, spare-time, open-ended study of 'liberal' subjects over a period of years. Little of this activity now remains, partly because of the expansion of provision, with the emphasis now on shorter courses and accreditation (see the discussion of adult and continuing in Chapter 3, and of accreditation in Chapter 7).

The terms 'liberal' and 'vocational' are, of course, imprecise, emotional and ideological. Just as, at the level of the individual, we may conceive of the same learning experience as being vocational for one learner but non-vocational for another (e.g. an 18 year old and a retired person following the same degree course), so may advocates of these two apparently opposed positions label provision as it suits their cause:

> The phrase 'liberal education' has today become something of a slogan which takes on different meanings according to its immediate context. It usually labels a form of education of which the author approves, but beyond that its meaning is often negatively derived. Whatever else a liberal education is, it is *not* a vocational education, *not* an exclusively scientific education, or *not* a specialist education in any sense.
>
> (Hirst 1974, p. 30, original emphasis).

Following this view, liberal and vocational become defined in terms of each other, or, rather, in terms of distorted and partial perceptions of each other. It is rather like a two-party political system, where government and opposition alternate, and may change their policies, but remain united in their continuing rejection of each other's positions, whatever they are.

These differences do have real consequences, however, for the nature of the education and training opportunities made available, so it is important to try and understand what lies behind them. For one author, liberal education is characterized by the following features:

1. What should be learnt is rooted firmly within intellectual disciplines.
2. To be educated is to be initiated into these disciplines. . .
3. The point or the value of the apprenticeship into the intellectual traditions, through which we come to understand and shape our experience, requires no further justification than reference to their own intrinsic value. . .
4. That initiation is a hard and a laborious task. . .
5. The control and the direction of that conversation, and thus of the initiation into it, must lie in the hands of those who are authorities within it.

(Pring 1993, pp. 54–5)

The same author sees vocational education in these terms:

1. The value of the educational encounter between teacher and student lies partly in the external purposes which it serves. . .
2. Therefore, the curriculum must be planned in terms of specific objectives which arise . . . from an analysis of what the economy needs or what skills certain occupations demand. . .
3. The content of the curriculum . . . must be relevant to industry and commerce.
4. The context of learning must be, as far as possible, in a realistic economic setting.
5. The educational experience as a whole should foster attitudes and dispositions such as entrepreneurship and enterprise. . .
6. People from outside the academic and educational communities must be partners in the establishment of these objectives and in assessing whether or not they have been reached.

(Pring 1993, p. 62)

These characterizations are supported in other recent discussions of the concepts (e.g. Barrow and Milburn 1990; Williams 1994).

However, these kinds of lists are inevitably rather stereotypical, and tend to buttress the oppositional view of liberal and vocational approaches to education. Thus, we might apply, in the former case, identifiers such as broad, general, long term, élitist, humanist, progressive, guided by professionals and 'useless'. Whereas, for the latter, we could come up with narrow, specific, short term, mass market, utilitarian, immediate, guided by practitioners and 'useful'.

Yet, just as the same learning experience may serve vocational and liberal purposes, however it may be designated by the provider, so are the concerns of avowedly liberal or vocational advocates similar in many ways. Thus, one of the surprising features of the rise of vocationalism over the last decade has been the extent to which it has been accepted, and even endorsed and welcomed, by many academics and educators. While a cynical or sceptical commentator might argue that this is because they have been cowed into acceptance, it may also be recognized that at least some of the policy changes introduced have been useful in a more general educational sense.

Similarly, many of those involved in the delivery of explicitly vocational education or training have shown their concern to broaden the learning experience:

> workers and managers in a post-industrial economy must learn primarily not new skills but new roles. But since training ... is based on the rigid separation of the training encounter from the natural world of work, it is unsuited as a process for helping people learn new roles and develop new relationships.
>
> (Hirschham, *et al.* 1989, p. 185)

While the liberal/vocational distinction has real power, therefore, we should not let it blind us to other developments, distinctions and similarities.

FURTHER READING

Barrow, R and Milburn, G (1990) *A Critical Dictionary of Educational Concepts: an appraisal of selected ideas and issues in educational theory and practice.* Hemel Hempstead, Harvester Wheatsheaf, second edition.
    Contains general discussions of most of the concepts considered in this chapter, but from a primarily school-based perspective.

Campanelli, P, Channell, J, McAulay, L, Renouf, A and Thomas, R (1994) *Training: an exploration of the word and the concept with an analysis of the implications for survey design*. Sheffield, Employment Department.
  Detailed analysis of understandings of the concept, using linguistic analysis, with substantial methodological implications.

Dearden, R (1984) 'Education and training'. *Westminster Studies in Education*, 7, pp. 57–66.
  Short, accessible, jargon free and considered treatment.

Jarvis, P (1990) *An International Dictionary of Adult and Continuing Education*. London, Routledge.
  A useful general source which includes brief analyses of many of the concepts included in this and later chapters.

Lawton, D and Gordon, P (1993) *Dictionary of Education*. Sevenoaks, Hodder and Stoughton.
  Useful for gaining a rapid introduction into many contemporary British educational issues, with a school-based emphasis.

Pring, R (1993) 'Liberal education and vocational preparation', pp. 49–78 in R Barrow and P White (eds) *Beyond Liberal Education: essays in honour of Paul Hirst*. London, Routledge.
  A recent example of the English philosophy of education school of writing.

Chapter 2

International concepts

THE INTERNATIONALIZATION OF ADULT EDUCATION AND TRAINING

The four concepts discussed in this chapter – lifelong education, recurrent education, the learning organization and the learning society – are grouped together because they jointly illustrate the post-Second World War growth in international thinking, policy-making and cooperation in the arenas of adult education and training. These developments have reflected the increased globalization of economies, society and technology. They have been reflected in the somewhat competitive work of a number of international organizations; notably the United Nations Educational, Scientific and Cultural Organization (UNESCO), the Organization for Economic Cooperation and Development (OECD), the Council of Europe, the International Labour Office and the World Bank.

With the exception of the learning organization (which became prominent only in the 1980s), these concepts were developed during the 1960s and 1970s, though they all have earlier antecedents. There were at least three main reasons for their articulation at this time: the increasing pace of economic, social and technological change; the perception that existing education and training practices and provision were inadequate to cope; and the belief that educational opportunities should be available to all. The concepts were developed against a backcloth of critical debate regarding the role of formal institutions and curricula, led by influential writers such as Freire and Illich (Freire 1972; Illich 1973).

With the hindsight which twenty or thirty years provides, some of these discussions may now seem to lack practical purchase, and to convey undue optimism about the possibility for democratic change based on reasoned argument and widespread participation in education and training. The associated structures of the welfare state, interventionist government and supranational organization have all come in for a good deal of criticism in the last two decades. Yet the concepts discussed in this chapter have not gone away; indeed, the fourth of them, the learning society, is currently enjoying something of a return to popularity.

LIFELONG EDUCATION

The idea, or ideal, of lifelong education (and/or lifelong learning) was adopted as a 'master concept' by the UNESCO in 1970 (Coombs 1968; Dave 1976; Fauré *et al.* 1972; Kallen 1979; Lengrand 1989). Its origins have been traced back to the writings of Dewey, Lindeman and Yeaxlee in the early twentieth century (Jarvis 1995). In essence, lifelong education, like the other concepts discussed in this chapter, argues for a rejection of a model of education which is confined to childhood, adolescence and early adulthood: frequently reviled and rather offensively labelled in the literature as the 'front-end' model. Instead, education is portrayed as being available throughout life, as needed and desired, for everyone.

The concept of permanent education was advanced at the same time by the Council of Europe (Council of Europe 1973, 1975). This concept had its origins in the French notion of *éducation permanente*, and is little used outside francophone countries. It is now regarded as essentially synonymous with lifelong education (see, for example, the definitions contained in Jarvis 1990), and will not, therefore, be discussed separately in this chapter.

The implications of lifelong education have been usefully summarized by one of its main proponents in the following fashion:

Lifelong education, conceptualised as a means for facilitating lifelong learning, would
1. last the whole life of each individual;
2. lead to the systematic acquisition, renewal, upgrading and completion of knowledge, skills and attitudes, as became necessary in response to the constantly changing

conditions of modern life, with the ultimate goal of promoting the self-fulfilment of each individual;
3. be dependent for its successful implementation on people's increasing ability and motivation to engage in self-directed learning activities;
4. acknowledge the contribution of all available educational influences including formal, non-formal and informal.

(Cropley 1980, pp. 3–4)

Three key features of the concept may be unpacked from this quotation and similar accounts (e.g. Gelpi 1979; Lengrand 1975). First, lifelong education is seen as building upon and affecting all existing educational providers, including both schools and institutions of higher education (Knapper and Cropley 1985; Williams 1977). Second, it extends beyond the formal educational providers to encompass all agencies, groups and individuals involved in any kind of learning activity (see the discussion of formal, non-formal and informal education in Chapter 3). Third, it rests on the belief that individuals are, or can become, self-directing, and that they will see the value in engaging in lifelong education.

There is, however, no 'standard' model of what a lifelong education system might look like. As Cropley himself admits (1979, p. 1), it is rather a slippery concept, which may be attractive to, and applied in different ways by, a wide variety of interests: 'Both totalitarian and liberal regimes express their support for lifelong education, as do technologically more developed as well as technologically less developed societies.'

Similarly, lifelong educational principles may be used to develop different curricula, for example vocational or non-vocational (see the section 'vocational or liberal?' in Chapter 1). Thus, one study of lifelong learning practices in over 30 companies and 200 higher education institutions in western Europe notes that:

If the main responsibility for lifelong learning is taken by industry, the focus is on training. It is initiated and financed by the company and has company goals. In lifelong learning programmes which are initiated by [educational] institutions, paid for by society or by the individual, the adult student's personal goal is often involved.

(Otala 1992, p. 21)

Clearly, while a good deal of progress has been made, no society has yet achieved the kind of educational or learning system advocated by UNESCO – not the USA, with its mass educational system built on a mix of public support and private investment; not Sweden, with its traditions of community and social provision, and its study circle model, though it has perhaps come closest; certainly not the failed Soviet system. While some of the richer nations are much more advanced in this respect than others, in all cases substantial proportions of the population remain excluded, uninvolved or under-involved in education (see, for example, OECD 1992; UNESCO 1989).

There are, of course, both theoretical and practical objections to the idea of lifelong education. Some writers have noted the way in which its proponents tend to equate education with learning, making little distinction between different forms or levels (Lawson 1982). Others have argued that the concept adds little to the notion of adult education (Wain 1987, 1993). Even its leading advocates have been forced to admit that the concept is rather vague and lacking in coherence: 'The vagueness of the concept of lifelong education disappears when it is translated into experience and practice' (Gelpi 1979, volume 1, p. 1). This vagueness stems partly from the use of the concept not just in differing societies and for varying curricula, but also in reference to a wide range of ideas:

> The term 'lifelong education' has been used in recent education literature variously to advocate or denote the function of education as being: the preparation of individuals *for* the management of their adult lives, the distribution of education *throughout* individual lifespans, the educative function *of* the whole of one's life experience, and the identification of education *with* the whole of life.
>
> (Bagnall 1990, p. 1, original emphasis)

The practical objections to the idea of lifelong education are just as telling. At the system level, financial and structural concerns appear paramount. It is, of course, a characteristic of conceptual development that little attention is typically given to pragmatic concerns like costs, but this ignorance in most writing about lifelong education does appear significant (and contrasts with writings about recurrent education – see below – where the economic linkages have always been more explicit). After all, the kind of changes envisaged in establishing a system of lifelong education do have massive financial implications, with no necessary economic benefit in return.

Structurally, the balance to be changed by the introduction of lifelong education can be seen as being that between education, work (or employment) and certain kinds of 'non-work', principally leisure and retirement. Education is being shifted from its dominant position in early life, to be combined with work and non-work in adult life.

This strategy may be challenged, particularly on the grounds that it presents a 'male' view of life and career (see the section on career in Chapter 4). Women are commonly involved in other kinds of 'non-work', such as caring for children and older people. They also form the basis of the part-time, and low paid, labour force. In practice, the option to combine educational participation with work, retirement, leisure or domestic responsibility may only be open to a limited number of adults: those with the right background who have the necessary support (Blaxter and Tight 1994).

National surveys continue to indicate that, in Britain as in other countries, the majority of adults are not involved in education, primarily because they lack support, interest or motivation (Sargant 1991). Those that are, and are responding to the opportunities and challenges which lifelong learning presents, still readily come up with lists of the financial, situational, institutional and attitudinal barriers to their effective and continuing participation.

RECURRENT EDUCATION

Recurrent education was sponsored as a concept in the 1970s by the OECD (Centre for Educational Research and Innovation 1973, 1975). Lifelong education appears to express a general ideal, which may then be interpreted in varied fashions. Recurrent education, on the other hand, suggests an alternating pattern for practice, which some have seen as a means for implementing lifelong education:

> The essence of the recurrent education proposition ... is the distribution of education over the lifespan of the individual in *a recurring way*. This means a break with the present

practice of a long, uninterrupted pre-work period of full-time schooling, which has been described as a 'front-end' model. It also implies the alternation of education with other activities, of which the principal would be work, but which might also include leisure and retirement. One of its essential potential outcomes is to make it possible for the individual to abandon the unalterable education–work–leisure–retirement sequence and to enable him [sic] to mix and alternate these activities within the limits of what is socially possible and in accordance with his own desires and aspirations.

(Council of Europe 1973, p. 7, original emphasis)

One of the early members of the Association for Recurrent Education (recently renamed the Association for Lifelong Learning!) identified twelve 'features which might be deemed essential for a recurrent education system' (Houghton 1974, p. 7). These were ordered under the headings of availability, access and relevance. His analysis, which has been labelled 'radical' by some commentators (Jarvis 1995; Lawson 1977), argued for the greatest possible choice, variety and flexibility. It also stressed the aim of producing autonomous learners or groups of learners.

The concept of recurrent education has been used as the basis for a range of both empirical studies (e.g. Jourdan 1981; Tuijnman 1989) and theoretical analyses (e.g. Rubenson 1977, 1987). It has also, in contrast to lifelong education, been the focus for much discussion regarding how such a system might be financed (e.g. Levin and Schütze 1983). This is perhaps not surprising, given the implications embedded within the concept for employment policy. Much practical attention has thus been given to the introduction and evaluation of different schemes of paid education leave, which enable those in employment to have time off for studying (Bengtsson 1989). With such a focus, the concept has obvious links with that of the learning organization (see below).

While recurrent education possibly remains more of a live concept than lifelong education, there are no large-scale examples of its achievement, and its advocates tend now to couch their analyses in terms of realism:

For recurrent education and training to be widely perceived as relevant by young people would depend upon at least three basic conditions being met. First, there would have to be employment opportunities readily available for those who complete compulsory school and who do not wish immediately to pursue further education and training. Second, career ladders and training opportunities would have to be provided in conjunction with such jobs. Third, participation in, and completion of, education and training programmes at a later point would have to provide occupational advancement and income commensurate with degrees or professional qualifications acquired in the traditional fashion, i.e. prior to entry to the labour force. These conditions are still far from being met.

(Schütze and Istance 1987, pp. 18–19)

The problems seem obvious: many economies remain in recession, many employers can see little advantage in enabling their employees to engage in more general education or training, many states have moved away from the interventionist policies which characterised the 1960s and 1970s. Few individuals are in the position to be able to afford the risk of engaging in a personal recurrent education strategy, while the benefits to them of doing so remain unproven.

THE LEARNING ORGANIZATION

The idea of the learning organization arises, like those of lifelong and recurrent education, from concerns about change and survival. While the articulation of the concept took place as late as the 1980s, at least three interrelated precursors for it (or pressures leading to it) may be identified.

The first of these derives from the concern of management consultants with how to encourage organizational as distinct from individual or group learning (Jones and Hendry 1994; Kim 1993). Organizational learning is seen as something greater than the sum of the bits of individual or group learning of which it is comprised: 'the intentional use of learning processes at the individual, group and system level to continuously transform the organization in a direction that is increasingly satisfying to its stakeholders' (Dixon 1994, p. 5). It represents an interaction between the organization's component parts, and the outside environment, to the benefit of the organization as a whole.

This school of thought is associated in particular with Argyris and Schön, and their work on organizational development, professionalism, theory of action and reflective practice (e.g. Argyris 1982, 1992; Argyris and Schön 1976, 1978; Schön 1983, 1988). Their writing on organizational learning is grounded within systems thinking:

> Organizational learning involves the detection and correction of error. When the error detected and corrected permits the organization to carry on its present policies or achieve its present objectives, then that error-detection-and-correction process is *single-loop* learning. . . . *Double-loop* learning occurs when error is detected and corrected in ways that involve the modification of an organization's underlying norms, policies and objectives.
>
> (Argyris and Schön 1978, pp. 2–3, original emphasis)

Argyris and Schön link their work to theoretical and empirical studies in a range of disciplines and sub-disciplines in the social sciences: social psychology, management theory, sociology, cybernetics, anthropology and politics.

The second line of thinking behind the learning organization has to do with the competitive necessities imposed by economic and technological changes, the drive towards permanent and sustained innovation, and consequent concerns with quality and value for money. These issues are reflected in the writings of modern management gurus like Lessem, Peters and Senge (Lessem 1991, 1993; Peters 1987; Senge 1990):

> In tracing the evolution of management over the past 50 years, you will find that history has repeated itself, albeit with some differences. Craftsmanship of traditional quality was displaced by mass production and marketing, which is now being replaced by intelligent manufacturing, of contemporary quality. Quality and learning have now displaced profitability and market share as the new managerial imperatives.
>
> (Lessem 1991, p. 3)

This line of thinking has found expression in the ideas of total quality management and its derivative, total quality learning (see the discussion of quality in Chapter 6). It underlies a number of recent initiatives, such as the Management Charter and Investors in People (Critten 1993; Rix, *et al.* 1994).

The third precursor for the current concern with the learning organization may be traced through changing industrial relations practice. Increasing numbers of companies operating in the less regulated industrialized economies – e.g. the United States and the United Kingdom – have sought to provide general educational and developmental opportunities for their employees (Forrester *et al.* 1993). These initiatives appear to be most widely developed in the car manufacturing industry (Chadwick 1993; Eurich 1990; Income Data Services 1994). They typically offer an annual sum for each employee to spend on some kind of learning activity, in addition to enhanced in-company training and development opportunities.

We may speculate upon the differing motivations of the managers and union representatives involved in agreeing such non-wage rewards: perhaps staff retention and motivation in the former case, and membership retention or expansion in the latter. We might also draw, not necessarily flattering, parallels with the learning or quality circles which have been developed within organizations in Sweden and other Nordic countries over many years. But such employee development initiatives have caught the imagination, and are now frequently seen as a key component of the learning organization.

As may be judged from the discussion so far, the idea of the learning organization applies many of the same ideas as lifelong and recurrent education, but at the organizational or company, rather than the individual or societal level:

> The Learning Company is a vision of what might be possible. It is not brought about simply by training individuals; it can only happen as a result of *learning at the whole organization* level. A Learning Company is an organization that facilitates the learning of all its members *and* continuously transforms itself.
>
> (Pedler *et al.* 1991, p. 1, original emphasis; see also Burgoyne, *et al.* 1994)

That reads as a rather top-down, managerially imposed view, and raises the questions of who participates in, and who has authority over, such learning. Much the same sentiments have been expressed, however, in a more democratic, bottom-up fashion:

> Learning organizations are characterized by total employee involvement in a process of collaboratively initiated, collabo-

ratively conducted, collectively accountable change directed
towards shared values or principles.

(Watkins and Marsick 1992, p. 118)

A third definition appears to offer elements of both of these
approaches:

A learning organization is one that has a climate that accel-
erates individual and group learning. Learning organizations
teach their employees the critical thinking process for understanding what it does and why it does it. These individuals
help the organization itself to learn from mistakes as well as
successes. As a result, they recognize changes in their environment and adapt effectively. Learning organizations can be seen
as a group of empowered employees who generate new
knowledge, products and services; network in an innovative
community inside and outside the organization; and work
towards a higher purpose of service and enlightenment to the
larger world.

(Marquardt and Reynolds 1994, p. 22)

The last phrase here sounds a little too altruistic. One might also
criticize the use of the term 'employees', where 'workers' would
allow a more general interpretation. These authors, linking the
idea of the learning organization to globalization, go on to identify a model for the global learning organization. They list eleven
essential organizational elements for global learning: appropriate
structures, a corporate learning culture, empowerment, envi-
ronmental scanning, knowledge creation and transfer, quality,
strategy, supportive atmosphere, teamwork and networking, and
vision.

Despite the high demands thus placed on becoming and
remaining a learning organization, many organizations have
been held up as examples, or at least as aspirants. These have
included, in the UK, Nabisco, Rover, Sheerness Steel and Sun
Alliance (Jones and Hendry 1992); and, further afield, General
Electric, Honda, Samsung and Xerox (Marquardt and Reynolds
1994).

A number of 'how to' publications now exist which aim to
demonstrate to managers and others how they can change their
organizations into learning organizations (Grundy 1994; Mayo
and Lank 1994). These are relatively clear in identifying the

prospective benefits to the main 'stakeholders' involved: the organization's customers, employees and shareholders. For example:

> Benefits for customers include ... making available to customers products and services that meet their evolving requirements more effectively than competitors ... the rate of innovation, not just in products and services, but in process adaptability and responsiveness.... Benefits for employees include... the ability to enhance both internal and external employability ... the opportunity for better job security ... a sense of self-respect.... Benefits for shareholders include ... differentiated human assets that have more value than those of the competition ... minimising voluntary losses of good people ... the reduction in layers of management ... the reduction of costs as continuous improvement yields continuous productivity increase ... the elimination of duplication and overlapping activity ... the ability to seize market opportunities through speed of adaptation and change ... the availability of the right people with the right skills in the right place at the right time.
>
> (Mayo and Lank 1994, pp. 9–13)

Given such an impressive list, one might wonder why all organizations are not seeking to become learning organizations as quickly as possible. Could it be that, in reality, the idea is as diaphanous and unrealizable as the idea of lifelong learning, reviewed earlier in this chapter. Or might it be that the learning organization is just one in a long line of 'latest management ideas', which come off the guru conveyer belt and on to the airport bookstalls most weeks.

The criticisms which may be levelled at the idea of the learning organization are many and various. Thus, amongst those that call themselves, or have been called, learning organizations, there are substantial variations in practice and experience. This can readily be demonstrated by, for example, the differences in who is included within the ambit of the learning organization: full-time staff, permanent staff, part-timers, all grades, customers, all plants, subsidiaries?

That listing raises another question about learning organizations, also highlighted by the definitions quoted. Is the learning organization about empowerment or exploitation? Is it in the business of creatively seeking the views and inputs of all its members, and giving them due credit and say in their use; or is it about squeezing as much value as possible out of each unit of production, with the resulting profits channelled in traditional ways? Does it emphasize organizational at the expense of individual learning, and transformation rather than incremental change (Mumford 1991)? Any concept which can encompass such radically differing viewpoints has major problems as well as considerable potential.

Then there is the issue – the 'bottom line' in management speak – of whether learning organizations actually do any better at their business than comparable 'non-learning' organizations. Here the evidence, as with that on general linkages between educational participation and economic productivity (see Chapter 4, particularly the sections on education and the economy and human capital), is both partial and difficult to interpret:

> The learning organization concept may provide the catalyst which is needed to push forward, in an holistic way, the many strands, ideas and values with which organizations must now concern themselves. . . . However, there are dangers. First, there is no detailed research work completed which can confirm or deny, over time, whether such ideas and practices genuinely create fitter and better organisations for both the people who work in them and the society they seek to serve. Secondly, there is the need to know how far the learning organisation concept is simply yet another 'vision' propounded by management and educational idealists or whether it is an idea capable of reality . . . the learning organisation can itself become the 'myth' which obscures its own nature and prevents advance towards other levels of learning and change.
>
> (Jones and Hendry 1992, pp. 58–9)

In other words, the consensual nature of idealizations such as the learning organization, which can become seen as the solution to problems of organizational survival and competitiveness, can act in counter-productive ways by denying the possibility of other solutions or progressions. In the final assessment:

> There is no perfect organization, for they are all peopled by fallible human beings; therefore, it is inevitable that

organisations make mistakes, get things wrong and suffer setbacks. . . . It is the way in which organisations respond to the normal features of the modern world and the lessons learnt from the experience that qualifies them for the title 'learning organisation'. It is not what they do, but how they do it.

(Dale 1993, p. 22)

THE LEARNING SOCIETY

While the learning society has only recently become the subject of considerable debate in the UK, it has a longer history in other countries which have a post-war tradition of greater educational participation. These include, for example, Canada, New Zealand, Sweden and the USA (Boshier *et al.* 1980; Carnegie Commission on Higher Education 1973; Commission on Post-secondary Education in Ontario 1972; Husen 1974, 1986).

In those societies the advent of discussion on the learning society may be linked not just to lifelong and recurrent education, but also to the development of ideas like the post-industrial society and the information society (Bell 1973; Toffler 1970). In the UK, by contrast, the contemporary connections are as much with the issues of active citizenship and the learning polity (Hayes, *et al.* 1995).

The learning society was recently defined in a briefing paper by the United Kingdom Economic and Social Research Council (ESRC) in the following terms:

A learning society would be one in which all citizens acquire a high quality general education, appropriate vocational training and a job (or series of jobs) worthy of a human being while continuing to participate in education and training throughout their lives. A learning society would combine excellence with equity and would equip all its citizens with the knowledge, understanding and skills to ensure national economic prosperity and much more besides. . . . Citizens of a learning society would, by means of their continuing education and training, be able to engage in critical dialogue and action to improve the quality of life for the whole community and to ensure social integration as well as economic success.

(ESRC 1994, p. 2)

This definition suggests the potentially all-encompassing nature of the learning society, which spans both vocational concerns (the link between education and economy) and quality of life issues (the link between education and personal and social development). Others might, of course, define the learning society rather more narrowly, focusing on just one of these poles of interest. As defined here, the concept clearly builds upon the notions of lifelong learning and the learning organization, and makes use of the ideas of productivity and change.

There are a number of tensions apparent within existing discussions on the learning society:

'The learning society' is an ambiguous term. It is descriptive, pointing to . . . complexities and underlining the centrality of change; it is analytical, suggesting the possibility that modern society . . . may be . . . continuing to learn about itself and steering itself along its chosen path; it is normative, urging the need for learning to have a high profile at both the individual and the societal level; and it is ontological, making a statement about the fundamental nature of modern society and pointing to the centrality of rationality. On each interpretation . . . education emerges as the key institution in modern society, but education conceived in terms broader than curricula framed by the academic community for young people.

(Barnett 1994, p. 70)

Yet, though the concept suggests a concern with the productive (in both senses) learning of all members of society, many of those writing on the topic have focused largely on school education (e.g. Husen 1974, 1986; Ranson 1992, 1994). Further, as the following two quotes illustrate, there is a division between the analysts and the visionaries:

Only poets and science fiction writers have imagined what a learning society would look like and how it would differ from today's world.

(Ainley 1994, p. 156)

modern statecraft is becoming little more than the proper management of learning.

(Thomas 1991, p. 160)

Both of these statements may be criticized, but the second one seems particularly wide of the mark. They do, however, confirm that the learning society should be seen as in part a description and in part an aspiration. Furthermore, they suggest that the idea of the learning society can be addressed on a number of levels: as a set of practices, as a policy blueprint, and as a myth advanced for political purposes (Hughes and Tight 1995).

Seen as a set of practices, at least three interpretations have been placed on the concept:

1. The learning society as an *educated society*, committed to active citizenship, liberal democracy and equal opportunities . . .
2. The learning society as a *learning market*, enabling institutions to provide services for individuals as a condition for supporting the competitiveness of the economy. . .
3. The learning society as *learning networks*, in which learners adopt a learning approach to life, drawing on a wide range of resources to enable them to develop their interests and identities.

(Edwards 1995, p. 187, original emphasis)

While the first and third of these interpretations have clear resonances with the ideals of lifelong education, as advanced in the 1960s and 1970s, it is the second, Edwards argues, which is currently dominant. This reflects the emphasis of present policy on the perceived need, in an increasingly competitive global economy, for the effective development and availability of all human resources. Yet, at least in the definition quoted earlier, the concern for the growth of the individual and the community still remains. So once again, as in the case of the learning organization, there is a conflict within the concept between top-down and bottom-up approaches.

While this broader vision of the learning society can be seen as an improvement on strict vocationalism, it does, therefore, represent something of an unhappy and unstable compromise. As a banner under which a diversity of interests – politicians, educators, industrialists – can gather, the learning society embodies an alliance between state, professions and capital. Such an alliance seems likely to marginalize the interests of the individual in pursuing learning for personal self-fulfilment.

Most of the criticisms which have been levelled at both lifelong education and the learning organization also apply to the

learning society. To their credit, in their briefing paper the ESRC
went on to question the notion of the learning society:

> Some of the claims made on behalf of the learning society need
> to be subjected to empirical test; for example, does learn-ing
> pay? does it empower and enable? does it help to equalise life
> chances? Will the purposes of education and training for the
> learning society need to encompass more then selection,
> socialisation, and minimal levels of literacy and numeracy in
> preparation for the world of work? What changes in education
> and training will be needed for all to participate fully in the
> learning society? Is there a set of values or guiding principles
> underpinning the notion of a learning society which need to
> be made explicit if a culture of education and training is to be
> created in the UK? What would a coherent and coordinated
> policy to help the UK become a learning society look like?
>
> (ESRC 1994, p. 4)

Other commentators have pointed out the vast disparity between
the rhetoric and present reality. Thus, the National Institute of
Adult Continuing Education (NIACE) of England and Wales
commissioned a survey which found that only 10 per cent of
those aged 17 or more were currently studying anything. Some
24 per cent had studied within the last 3 years, but the majority,
52 per cent, claimed not to have studied at all since they left
school. The NIACE's conclusion was that: 'There is still a massive
gap between the government's vision of a learning society where
people invest in updating their own skills throughout their lives,
and the actual amount of learning adults undertake' (NIACE
1994, p. 1).

Clearly, participation rates do not match the rhetoric associated with the concept of the learning society. On the basis of
empirical evidence, there is little to support the notion that we
have already achieved in the United Kingdom, in any real sense,
a learning society. A rather larger claim might be made for some
other countries, but even in these cases, it is at best a partial
vision of the learning society that is being achieved, with many
still excluded. And when consideration is given to the embedded
nature of the structural inequalities associated with access to
education and training in all countries, we are left with a sense
of disillusionment that a learning society in its fullest sense will
ever be achieved.

IDEALS AND FASHIONS

A number of conclusions may be drawn from this analysis of four international concepts relating to adult education and training. Three of these will be briefly discussed here.

First, we may question just how different the concepts are in their meanings and applications. Even a brief engagement with some of the sources quoted in this chapter will show the reader how common it is to find the concepts linked together, or even defined in terms of each other. Thus, recurrent education may be viewed simply as one strategy for implementing lifelong education, while both have a central role within the learning society. Similarly, while the idea of the learning organization may seem to be somewhat distinct from the other three – in its specific concern with organizations – it can be seen as an essential element of them, focusing on the second level in the individual/organization/society hierarchy.

A more precise analysis might see lifelong education and recurrent education as alternative means for achieving the same end: the greater involvement of adults in education and training. But, whereas recurrent education suggests an alternation of education with other activities in adult life, lifelong education implies an almost continuous combination of educational involvement with other activities or roles. Yet neither of these models is likely to suit everybody and every circumstance, and we are nowhere near creating a comprehensive system of adult education and training. So we might simply treat these concepts as overlapping alternative patterns to be used as needs suggest and circumstances allow.

Second, the realism of these concepts as models for national or organizational systems of provision has to be questioned. We have already argued that none of them have been achieved on a system-wide basis, but we might also consider whether they are, by their very nature, achievable or not. It has been argued that these concepts are both utopian in nature and have the characteristics of myths (Hughes and Tight 1995; Tight 1994). This was recognized at the time of their development by at least some of their proponents:

> reference to the concept met with many reservations, if not hostile attitudes. Some educators expressed the view that lifelong education was nothing more than a new term to

designate adult education and that its use led to confusion. Others, while recognizing the rationality underlying the concept, looked upon it as Utopian, reaching far beyond the possibilities of implementation of a great number of countries.

(Lengrand 1989, p. 8)

Ideals are, of course, widely used to inform and drive policy development. But, if they remain well beyond the possibility of achievement, their effectiveness may be limited. Though the concepts of lifelong and recurrent education are still discussed and used in the literature (see, for example, Fordham 1992; Haggis 1991), they appear with far less frequency than they did ten or twenty years ago.

Thus, third, and finally, the history of these concepts appears to tell us something about changing fashions in adult education and training, as well as, on a larger scale, in political ideology. At the present time, discussion is likely to make use of more mundane and apparently neutral labels such as 'adult education', 'continuing education' or 'training' (see the discussion of adult and continuing in Chapter 3). Or, at the inspirational edge, it is likely to make use of the concepts of the learning organization and the learning society, which now seem largely to have overtaken and supplanted lifelong and recurrent education.

FURTHER READING

Fauré, E, Herrera, F, Kaddowa, A, Lopes, H, Petrovsky, A, Rahnema, M and Ward, F (1972) *Learning To Be: the world of education today and tomorrow*. Paris, UNESCO/Harrap.
Well-written policy statement, detailing the aims and the possible reality of lifelong education.

Forrester, K, Payne, J and Ward, K (eds) (1993) *Developing a Learning Workforce: conference proceedings*. Leeds, University of Leeds, Department of Adult Continuing Education.
Useful collection of papers on employee development schemes in Britain and North America.

Jarvis, P (1995) *Adult and Continuing Education: theory and practice*. London, Routledge, second edition.
Standard, and recently updated, text which contains a useful chapter analysing the various concepts discussed in this chapter.

Jones, A and Hendry, C (1992) *The Learning Organization: a review of literature and practice*. London, HRD Partnership.
Useful review of the literature up until the early 1990s.

Lawson, K (1982) *Analysis and Ideology: conceptual essays on the education of adults*. Nottingham, University of Nottingham Department of Adult Education.
    Collection of critical assessments of conceptual developments, including lifelong and recurrent education.
Mayo, A and Lank, E (1994) *The Power of Learning: a guide to gaining competitive advantage*. London, Institute of Personnel and Development.
    Very positive account of the learning organization and how to create it.
Schütze, H and Istance, D (eds) (1987) *Recurrent Education Revisited: modes of participation and financing*. Stockholm, Almqvist and Wiksell.
    Interesting consideration of many of the practical issues underlying the introduction of a system of recurrent education.
Titmus, C (ed.) (1989) *Lifelong Education for Adults: an international handbook*. Oxford, Pergamon.
    Substantial book which contains a number of essays on lifelong education, recurrent education and related concepts.

Chapter 3

Institutional concepts

THE INSTITUTIONAL FRAMEWORK

All countries or systems have an established institutional and legal framework which structures the ways in which adult education and training are provided. Of course, many organizations which are not designated as educational or training institutions are also involved in this provision, and the greater amount of adult learning in its broadest sense takes place outside of all such institutional arrangements. Nevertheless, it remains the case that those organizations specifically or largely dedicated to adult education and training, particularly those of higher status, have a major influence on the overall patterns of provision and practice.

This chapter examines a series of linked concepts which have to do with the labelling, nature and organization of institutions whose sole or major purpose is the delivery of adult education and training. There is, perhaps not surprisingly, a good deal of variation here in both practice and terminology from country to country, and the terms chosen for discussion in this chapter undoubtedly reflect an anglocentric bias. All of the concepts examined are, however, in widespread and current use in a number of countries, if not wholly international in scope. All have equivalents, or near equivalents, in other, non-anglophone systems.

The concepts analysed in this chapter are:

- further and higher, two terms which together can be seen to cover all formal post-compulsory educational provision, but which make a distinction in terms of its level and/or nature;

- adult and continuing, also potentially all-encompassing terms for the post-compulsory educational phase, but which have narrower interpretations as well;
- community, a concept with a wealth of meanings which extends far beyond education and training, but in this context implies some form of local, comprehensive provision, often serving all age groups;
- formal, non-formal and informal, a threefold categorization which recognizes the importance of education, training and learning outside education and training institutions.

This group of concepts may be viewed as collectively – or in some cases, and by some interpretations, individually – covering the entirety of the post-compulsory, post-initial, post-secondary or post-school educational and training provision available within a country. The extent of this provision, and the boundaries to and within it, vary from country to country and system to system.

Part of this variation is suggested by, and has to do with, the use of the labels post-compulsory, post-initial, post-secondary and post-school to delimit, in terms of institutions as well as age groups, adult from non-adult education and training. These four expressions may be briefly defined as follows:

- post-compulsory education or training takes place after the individual has passed the minimum school leaving age (i.e. is, in some sense, 'voluntarily' involved in education or training);
- post-initial education or training takes place after the individual has finished continuous full-time (i.e. initial) education;
- post-secondary education or training takes place after the completion of the secondary school phase (i.e. tertiary education or training and beyond);
- post-school education or training takes place after leaving school.

The age at which compulsory, initial, secondary or school education ends is somewhat different in different countries, and may indeed vary within countries (as it does, for example, within the UK between England and Scotland). It will also vary quite significantly from individual to individual. Thus, in England, compulsory education currently ends at age 16; secondary education may end at any age from 16 onwards, but would not normally last beyond 19 years; school education ends at between 16 and 19 years; and initial education finishes at any age between 16 years and the mid-twenties, depending on whether the individual concerned studies for a first degree, higher degree or further qualification.

Consequently, the age at which further, higher, adult or continuing education and training begins will also vary. The position is further complicated by the existence of overlaps between institutions labelled compulsory, initial, secondary or school and those labelled further, higher, adult or continuing. These overlaps are made manifest in, indeed are regarded as a strength of, the field of community education, which often seeks to serve both adult and non-adult clients, and those who missed, were excluded from or 'failed' school.

These labels may also be culturally specific. Thus, in the USA, 'school' has a more generic meaning, and may be applied colloquially to almost any formal educational institution, including universities and colleges; a usage which would likely cause confusion or offence in the UK.

FURTHER AND HIGHER

Further education and higher education are most often distinguished in terms of the level and nature of the education offered, with higher education being typified as the more advanced and less immediately vocational of the two. Alternatively, higher education may be seen as a specialized sub-set of further education.

Taken together, the two concepts may be broadly interpreted to include all post-compulsory or post-school (though not necessarily post-initial or post-secondary) education and training taking place in educational or training institutions. Such a definition would not be precise, however, as it ignores the institutional and age group overlaps already alluded to.

In England, further education may begin at the age of 16 for those who leave school then, or it may be entered at any later age or, indeed, never. Similarly, while higher education might begin at the age of 18, after school and/or further education, it might also be delayed or never entered.

Further education institutions, which in some ways may be seen as intermediary between school and higher education, may offer courses found elsewhere in schools and universities, with which they may then be in direct competition. They represent a potentially all-encompassing institutional form, perhaps including what would otherwise be the local school sixth form (as a tertiary college), and offering a range of degree programmes franchised from or validated by a university (Cantor and Roberts 1986; Hill 1994). Similarly, higher education institutions may provide some further education courses, and even, in some cases, offer provision which would normally be located in schools (a feature which was more common before the Second World War: see, for example, Bell and Tight 1993).

While accepting that the age at which further education and higher education begin is blurred by different national, institutional and, most especially, individual practices, we also have to recognize the varied national usages of the terms further and higher. Here, we may contrast the usage in England and Wales with that in the United States.

In the early 1970s, the Carnegie Commission on Higher Education in the United States defined further and higher education, seen together as the components of post-secondary education, in the following terms:

Higher education as oriented toward academic degrees or broad occupational certificates. It takes place on college or university campuses or through campus-substitute institutions, such as the 'open university' with its 'external degrees'.

Further education as oriented toward more specific occupational or life skills, rather than academic degrees. It takes place in many noncampus environments – industry, trade unions, the military, proprietary vocational schools, among others.

(Carnegie Commission on Higher Education 1973, p. 3)

The distinction made here is based not on age, but on the nature and institutional location of the studies undertaken. There is also an implicit, though by no means hard and fast, suggestion of a difference in terms of level (and perhaps status) and extent of commitment. Thus, higher education may be seen as operating at a 'higher' level, demanding a lengthier period of study, and involving more abstract and theoretical learning. This distinction also embodies elements of the vocational or liberal split discussed elsewhere (see the examination of 'vocational or liberal?' in Chapter 1), with further education portrayed as the more explicitly vocational form of provision.

Yet, in institutional terms, as already suggested, the distinction in provision and roles is not that clear cut. Some universities and colleges offer, as part of their overall provision, forms of education and training which fit the Carnegie definition of further education. Similarly, some institutions other than those identified offer academic degree programmes, including, increasingly, some industrial and commercial companies.

In England and Wales (Scotland has a somewhat different system of educational provision), on the other hand, further and higher education have a rather different, though at root similar, meaning. Here, further education was initially defined by the 1944 Education Act, and subsequently modified and rephrased by the 1988 Education Reform Act as:

(a) full- and part-time education and training for persons over compulsory school age (including vocational, social, physical and recreational training); and (b) organised leisure-time occupation provided in connection with the provision of such education.

(quoted in Hill 1994, p. 21)

This definition is clearly age related, though persons over the compulsory school age might study elsewhere than in further education institutions. There is no specific mention of the level of study, so further education could be seen as encompassing higher education. In practice, however, further education and higher education institutions have long been treated separately and differently by the British government. Interestingly, the definition makes greater reference to liberal ('social', 'physical', 'recreational', 'leisure-time') than to vocational forms of provision.

There is no similar, generally accepted, legalistic definition of what is meant by higher education (or even of the more specific term 'university', which remains more popular). Nevertheless, most British discussions treat this term as if it were fairly unproblematic. Much more attention is given to what higher education institutions do, or do not do, than to what higher education is in any more absolute sense (e.g. Bligh 1990; Committee on Higher Education 1963; Tight 1989). Hence, most available definitions appear to be superficially straightforward; for example:

> In the United Kingdom, 'higher education' is taken generally to refer to advanced courses provided mainly though not exclusively by the universities, polytechnics, colleges or institutes of higher education. 'Advanced' in this context usually means beyond A-level standard, and in fact entrance requirements are typically stated in terms of A levels.
>
> (Squires 1987, p. 128)

As in the case of the American interpretation, here the term is linked to particular institutional forms, much the same ones as selected in the United States.

These definitions are, however, rather circular in nature. Higher education is that which is provided mainly by universities and similar institutions: universities offer, either wholly or chiefly, higher education. There is nothing in either of the American or British definitions quoted here which tells us what it is about higher education which makes it 'higher'; or how it differs from 'lower' or 'not-so-high' education, other than simply by following on from it.

A few authors have, however, attempted to examine the meaning of the term in more depth:

> 'Higher education' is essentially a matter of the development of the mind of the individual student. It is not just any kind of development that the idea points to. An educational process can be termed higher education when the student is carried on to levels of reasoning which make possible critical reflection on his or her experiences, whether consisting of propositional knowledge or of knowledge through action. These levels of reasoning and reflection are 'higher', because they enable the student to take a view (from above, as it were) of what has been learned. Simply, 'higher education' resides in the higher-order states of mind.
>
> (Barnett 1990, p. 202)

This kind of reasoning takes us further and in a different direction, breaking away from the institutional or qualification-based focus of the definitions already quoted. It also provides some guidance as to how higher education might be identified at the individual level. Indeed, Barnett (1990, p. 203) goes on to specify six things which higher educational processes promote:

1. A deep understanding ... of some knowledge claims.
2. A radical critique ... of those knowledge claims.
3. A developing competence to conduct that critique in the company of others.
4. ... involvement in determining the shape and direction of that critique.
5. ... the capacity critically to evaluate his or her own achievements ...
6. The opportunity ... to engage in that inquiry in a process of open dialogue and cooperation.

(Barnett 1990, p. 203)

Such a definition is, in principle, applicable to all countries and systems; though this would, of course, rest upon a shared appreciation of what expressions like 'deep understanding', 'knowledge claims', 'radical critique' and 'competence' (see the sections on knowledge and competence in Chapter 6) mean.

ADULT AND CONTINUING

Both adult education and continuing education have contested – broader or narrower, traditional or modern, radical or conservative – meanings. While the latter concept is not in such wide use, the former has worldwide acceptance. The term adult, in its more general and personal sense, has already, of course, been discussed in Chapter 1. Here the focus is on what is meant, particularly in an institutional sense, by adult education or adult training.

In its more 'traditional' meaning, adult education refers not just to the age and status of its clients, but also encompasses the notion of participatory learning for its own sake and not for credit. As such, adult education is as much a movement as a set of institutions. It is often closely linked with the idea of liberal education, so that the term liberal adult education is in wide usage in some countries (see the discussion of 'vocational or liberal?' in Chapter 1). This interpretation of adult education has also been termed the 'great tradition', the five distinguishing characteristics of which have been identified as being:

(i) It is committed to a particular curriculum, to the humane or liberal studies.

(ii) Within this curriculum particular concern is shown for the social studies . . . its interest is in learning . . . as a means of understanding the great issues of life.

(iii) It demands from . . . students a particular attitude – the non-vocational attitude . . . and therefore examinations and awards . . . are deplored.

(iv) It combines democratic notions about equality of educational opportunity with . . . assumptions about the educability of normal adults.

(v) It . . . has found in small tutorial groups meeting for guided discussion over a fairly long period its most effective educational technique.

(Wiltshire 1956, pp. 88–9)

Even at the time this account was written, however, the great tradition was recognized as being in decline, and was looked back upon, with regret, as a largely pre-Second World War phenomenon. More recently, with changes in public policy and funding, the retreat away from the liberal conceptions of the great tradition has become more of a rout (Crombie and Harries-Jenkins 1983; McIlroy and Spencer 1988). Some reflections may still be seen, however, in contemporary 'radical' forms of adult education (Evans 1987; Thomas 1982; Ward and Taylor 1986), as well as in some kinds of community education (examined later in this chapter).

In its widest sense, the concept of adult education may be taken to refer to all education for adults. As such, it occupies, like further and higher education combined, the whole territory of post-compulsory provision, and may even be seen to extend beyond this to include less institutionalized forms of provision as well (Darkenwald and Merriam 1982; Groombridge 1983). For many practitioners, however, especially those from an older generation, the distinction between 'adult education', narrowly defined, and the broader context of 'education for adults' continues to have significance:

The 'education of adults' can . . . be seen to cover all forms of education (planned learning opportunities) for those over the age of 16 (or whatever), whether the student participants are treated as adults or . . . as if they were younger learners

– taught, that is, as if they were largely or completely igno-
rant of the subject being studied, without relevant experience,
unable to be relied upon to control their own learning, having
little or nothing to contribute to the learning process. 'Adult
education', by contrast, consists of all those forms of education that treat the student participants as adults – capable,
experienced, responsible, mature and balanced people.

(Rogers 1986, p. 17)

Many would reject both the straightforward distinctions between
adults and children suggested here (see the section on 'andragogy'
in Chapter 5), and the implied focus of attention on just one area
of the broad field of adult education and training. Yet the concept
of 'adult education' still carries a wealth of meanings and percep-
tual baggage, in the United Kingdom and elsewhere, which may
be seen to effectively limit its conceptual and practical usefulness:

> The term 'adult education' carries specific connotations in the
> United Kingdom which imply that it is specifically liberal
> education, and this also has a stereotype of being a middle
> class, leisure time pursuit. Underlying this implication is the
> idea that the adult's education has been completed and,
> during leisure time, the adult self-indulgently improves or
> broadens existing knowledge, skills or hobbies . . . it is hardly
> surprising that adult education is regarded as marginal.
>
> (Jarvis 1995, p. 20)

This quotation makes clear a very common view of adult education as an essentially spare-time activity. This activity is engaged
in for interest or amusement by individuals whose major role is
not that of a learner, but that of a worker, whether paid or
unpaid, to which role education makes little contribution.

The definition arrived at by the United Nations Educational,
Scientific and Cultural Organization (UNESCO) is, by contrast,
a good example of a broader and more 'modern' conceptualization of adult education:

> The term 'adult education' denotes the entire body of organ-
> ised educational processes, whatever the content, level, and
> method, whether formal or otherwise, whether they prolong
> or replace initial education in schools, colleges, and universi-
> ties, as well as in apprenticeship, whereby persons regarded
> as adult by the society to which they belong develop their

abilities, enrich their knowledge, improve their technical or professional qualifications, or turn them in a new direction and bring about changes in their attitudes and behaviour in the two-fold perspective of full personal development and participation in balanced and independent social, economic and cultural development.

> (quoted in Kidd and Titmus 1989, p. xxvii)

This definition may be compared with that given by another international body, the Organization for Economic Cooperation and Development (OECD):

> Adult Education refers to any learning activity or programme deliberately designed by a providing agent to satisfy any learning need or interest that may be experienced at any stage in his or her life by a person who is over the statutory school leaving age and whose principal activity is no longer in education. Its ambit, thus, spans non-vocational, vocational, general, formal and non-formal studies as well as education with a collective social purpose.

> (OECD 1977, p. 11)

Each of these definitions can be seen to encompass both training and education, vocational and non-vocational provision, study for qualifications and for its own sake, and educational provision outside expressly educational institutions as well as within. Their separate articulation can be seen as another example of the 'competition' between such international bodies in this area (see the section on the internationalization of adult education and training in Chapter 2).

The OECD definition is the broader of the two, stated in terms of learning activities rather than educational processes. While the UNESCO definition may be equated with post-initial education, the OECD's appears equivalent to post-compulsory education. The former stresses the joint purposes of national and individual development, and can be seen as relevant to developing as well as developed countries (see the discussion of development in Chapter 1). It also neatly avoids the problem of defining what it means to be an adult, by contextualizing it in terms of local societal perceptions.

The widespread use of the term continuing education has developed in the UK partly in response to the perceived restrictiveness of narrower interpretations of adult education, to which it may be seen as an alternative. It is also used partly in recognition of the changing audiences and curricula within education for adults. Thus university Departments of Adult Education, or Extra-Mural Studies – the equivalent of extension or external departments in other countries – have over the last decade changed their titles to Adult and Continuing Education, or just Continuing Education. Yet, as with adult education, there are broader and more restrictive definitions of the term in use.

The articulation of a wider role for continuing education can be seen in the work of the Advisory Council for Adult and Continuing Education (ACACE) during the late 1970s and early 1980s, which built on a number of earlier initiatives (e.g. Committee of Inquiry 1973). In their major report, the ACACE noted that:

> Our definition of continuing education is . . . a broad one. We do not think that it is useful to draw artifical boundaries between education and training, between vocational and general education, or between formal and informal systems of provision. We include systematic learning wherever it takes place: in libraries, in the work place, at home, in community groups and in educational institutions.
>
> (ACACE 1982, p. 2)

This definition would include the whole of further and higher education, in addition to a great variety of provision provided outside educational institutions, and much that took place outside institutions altogether. It may be contrasted with the very narrow approach to the concept at one time taken by the British government, which saw continuing education – in contrast to its non-vocational view of adult education – as being confined to post-experience vocational provision for those in employment (Department of Education and Science 1980). This would place its focus on mainly short and non-award-bearing courses, designed to update those working in professional, industrial or commercial contexts.

The broader conceptualization of continuing education has now, however, gained wider acceptance within the United Kingdom, though it is often, as already indicated, bracketed together with adult education as a joint or linked activity. Continuing education is now seen to be one of the main roles of both further and higher education institutions (e.g. National

Advisory Body 1984; Open University 1976; University Grants Committee 1984). The usage of the term is also extending in other, particularly anglophone, countries. For some, however, the term remains reactive rather than radical, lacking either the sense of tradition attached to adult education or the activist edge of community education: 'the concept appears to be a politically neutral one neither making reference or criticism of the initial education system nor implying any form of evalua-tion of the total contemporary educational system' (Jarvis 1995, p. 27).

COMMUNITY

'Community' is one of those evocative words which sounds innately appealing and worthwhile, conjuring up images of warmth, belonging and place, yet is very difficult to pin down as a useful or meaningful concept (Brookfield 1983, Plant 1974). As such, it is an ideological, and potentially a dangerous, term:

> *Community* can be the warmly persuasive word to describe an existing set of relationships, or the warmly persuasive word to describe an alternative set of relationships. What is most important, perhaps, is that unlike all other terms of social organisation (*state, nation, society,* etc) it seems never to be used unfavourably, and never to be given any positive opposing or distinguishing terms.
>
> (Williams 1988, p. 76, original emphasis)

A number of reviewers have identified a wide range of different meanings for the term 'community'. Thus, Clark identifies five main points of entry into the idea, viewing community as a human collective, as territory, as shared activities, as close-knit relationships, or as sentiment (Clark 1987). Similarly, Newman gives six common ways of interpreting the concept: community as the working class, as the quiescent poor, as the disadvan-taged, as the 'whole community', as the acceptable community, and as society (Newman 1979). He concludes that:

> There is probably no single, satisfactory definition of 'commu-nity'. But we misunderstand the word grossly if we appeal to the community as any kind of incontrovertible authority,

as if we assume that the community can be represented by a single cause. One of the clues to the meaning of 'community' lies in its utter *lack* of any statutory authority.

(Newman 1979, p. 209, original emphasis)

These varied interpretations have not, however, prevented the widespread use of the concept, in education and training as in other fields, in many different countries in both the developed and developing worlds (Poster and Kruger 1990; Poster and Zimmer 1992). In some countries, particularly in Latin America and Eastern Europe, the terms 'popular education' and 'folk education' may be used instead of, or in conjunction with, community education. In others, especially developing countries, non-formal education (see the next section) may be the preferred expression.

Naturally, these varied uses have different institutional expressions. Community colleges, for example, exist on both sides of the Atlantic, but the term is applied to different kinds of institutions. In the United States and Canada, community colleges are in the higher education sector, and offer sub-degree and degree-level study. Their nearest English equivalent would, therefore, be a further education college, outside the higher education sector.

In England, community colleges are far less widespread, but generally take the form of secondary schools which offer a range of adult education and recreational provision as well (Fairbairn 1971). In Scotland, the term community education is used more generally to refer to adult education, usually offered in association with youth and other community services (Scottish Education Department 1983). The common theme shared by these different institutional forms is their concern to recruit and serve a wide range of people: a community, though not necessarily the whole community.

The use of the term for educational purposes extends far beyond these examples, and has a lengthy history:

A survey of twentieth-century developments appears to reveal three major strands in the evolution of community education in Britain. First, the secondary school-based village/ community college movement pioneered by Henry Morris in Cambridgeshire; second, the trend towards community primary schooling in some urban areas following the Plowden

Report (1967) and experimentation in the Educational Priority Areas; third, innovative work in adult education and community development undertaken in some of the Home Office sponsored Community Development Projects in the late 1960s and early 1970s.

(Martin 1987, p. 22)

The first of these strands relates partly to the examples just discussed, of the community college and the community school. Like many other longer-standing movements, this 'school' of community education has its saints – Henry Morris in England, Charles Mott in the United States – its literature and its advocates: 'Community education is normally understood as the process of transforming schools and colleges into educational and recreational centres for all ages' (Fletcher 1989, p. 51; see also Fletcher 1980).

The second – in so far as it relates to adult education and training – and third strands identified by Martin embody the ideas of outreach and activism. Outreach is concerned with taking educational provision to where its clients are, that is outside of established educational institutions; while activism sees the educator's role as clearly political. The third strand, in particular, links to a more radical 'tradition' of adult education, which sees educators as being the servants of the disadvantaged, and adult education as being about engendering change (Hamilton 1992; Lovett et al. 1983).

Lovett himself has identified three main approaches within this strand, all of them explicitly linked to serving the working class:

there are three distinct 'models' of community education ... which reflect very different views about the nature of the problems facing the working class and the policies and strategies necessary to resolve them ... Community Organisation ... usually implies appointing outreach workers to work outside adult education institutions in working class communities. ... This ... model is in fact an extension of the liberal tradition in adult education ... Community Development ... takes a more active attitude. ... Community educators operate in local communities working on various local projects providing information, resources, advice and, when the occasion arises, research, education and training. ... Community Action ...

places greater stress on . . . learning through doing. There is more emphasis on the role of conflict in the resolution of local problems and the opportunities this provides for raising consciousness amongst those involved.

(Lovett 1982, pp. i–iii, original emphasis)

Lovett's own commitment is clearly to the last of these models, which demonstrates the strongest identification with, and commitment to, working-class communities. It also recognizes that any given community is unlikely to share a homogeneous view on a given issue. Communities, in other words, are groups which are not indifferent to each other's interests, but which are likely to contain conflicting interests.

Amidst all of these types, strands and models, what, if any, common themes may be identified? Another analyst, working within the Scottish tradition, has isolated the following:

Community Education:
1. is a life-long activity;
2. . . . that lays great emphasis upon the learner's active participation in learning and decision-making;
3. . . . that lays great stress upon the problems and needs of
people as starting points for learning . . .
4. . . . that can be identified as being based within identifiable
communities whether these be neighbourhoods or communities of interest. . . .
5. . . . that lays great stress upon the process of change as well
as the achievement of change in itself. . . .
6. is education yet claims to encompass more informal and
non-formal methods and contexts.

(McConnell 1982, p. 8)

This definition makes clear the links between community education and the concepts of lifelong education (see Chapter 2) and
non-formal and informal education (see the following section).
Reduced to these common conditions, however, there may seem
little implied by community education that is not included within
adult education, or within education in general. The ideas of
learner participation, starting from the problems and needs of
the learner, and educating for change, are found in many contemporary approaches to learning and education (see Chapter 5).
Once the idea of community itself is broadened to apply to either

an area or a common interest, most of the remaining distinctions seem to vanish. And with them goes a lot of the warmth and commitment carried by the concept as well.

FORMAL, NON-FORMAL AND INFORMAL

The notions of non-formal and informal education came to prominence during the 1960s and 1970s in international discussions on education. They may thus be related to the concepts of lifelong and recurrent education, which have similar origins (see Chapter 2). Yet, whereas the latter group of concepts have to do with the extension of education and learning throughout life, the former are about acknowledging the importance of education, learning and training which takes place outside recognized specialist educational institutions.

In this trilogy: 'Formal education is that provided by the education and training system set up or sponsored by the state for those express purposes' (Groombridge 1983, p. 6). The other two concepts, non-formal and informal education, were introduced with particular reference to the problems of developing countries (Coombs 1968, 1985). They are, however, also applicable to developed countries (e.g. Fordham *et al.* 1979), though in such cases they are more likely to be labelled as community education (see the previous section).

In developing countries, the formal educational system will typically only be available to, and/or used by, the minority of the adult population. In such circumstances, non-formal education, which encompasses all organised educational or training activity outside of the formal education system, may offer a cheaper and more accessible means for delivering needed learning. Non-formal education, while not constituting a parallel system, covers:

> any organised, systematic, educational activity, carried on outside the framework of the formal system, to provide selected types of learning to particular subgroups in the population, adults as well as children. Thus defined nonformal education includes, for example, agricultural extension and farmer training programmes, adult literacy programmes, occupational skill training given outside the formal system, youth clubs with substantial educational purposes, and

various community programmes of instruction in health, nutrition, family planning, cooperatives, and the like.

(Coombs and Ahmed 1974, p. 8)

A simpler definition has, however, been offered by the OECD: 'education for which none of the learners is enrolled or registered' (OECD 1977, p. 11). This stresses the location of non-formal education outside of educational institutions. There, it takes place under the auspices of organizations which do not need to mimic the more restrictive frameworks and accreditation systems of the formal sector.

The advantages of non-formal over formal education for contributing to national and personal development (see the discussion of development in Chapter 1) have been stressed by a number of authors:

In the context of new development strategies, non-formal education is being viewed as more relevant to the needs of the population, especially for those in the rural areas working in the traditional sector, since it attempts to focus on teaching people to improve their basic level of subsistence and their standards of nutrition and general health. . . . Further, since the non-formal education process usually requires the participation of its recipients in determining the nature and content of the educational programmes, these will always tend to focus on the needs and priorities of the communities.

(Fordham 1980, pp. 6–7)

Seen in these terms, non-formal education has clear linkages not just with ideas of community education, but more particularly with the practices of educators such as Freire (see the examination of conscientization in Chapter 5).

The third member of the trilogy considered in this section, informal education, may then be seen to cover all forms of learning not included in formal and non-formal education. Thus, it refers to:

The life-long process by which every individual acquires and accumulates knowledge, skills, attitudes and insights from daily experiences and exposure to the environment – at home, at work, at play: from the example and attitudes of family and friends; from travel, reading newspapers and books; or by listening to the radio or viewing films or television.

Generally, informal education is unorganised, unsystematic and even unintentional at times, yet it accounts for the great bulk of any person's total lifetime learning – including that of even a highly 'schooled' person.

(Coombs and Ahmed 1974, p. 8)

Here, there are close connections to the ideas of experiential, independent and self-directed learning (considered in Chapter 5).

TENSIONS, TRADITIONS AND DICHOTOMIES

Several themes may be seen running through the analysis of institutional concepts presented in this chapter.

One theme is that of tension. Thus, there are evident tensions between the institutional expressions of concepts and the concepts themselves. The labels 'adult' and 'community', to take two examples, are used differently by different institutions. There are also related tensions between institutional practices and the legal frameworks within which they operate, as exemplified in the overlaps between further and higher education.

Then there are the tensions between institutional forms and individual needs, such that particular adults may be using the same institutions at different ages and for varied reasons. All of these tensions have both spatial, in that usages vary from place to place and country to country, and temporal dimensions, in that the application of concepts has changed historically, as well.

A recognition of this variation provides a useful link to a second theme, that of 'tradition'. This word has been put in inverted commas not to signify its status as another concept, but to suggest the need for some caution in its use. For traditions are manufactured every day, and it is often the case that, when we refer to certain practices as being traditional, they are not of any great historical provenance (Hobsbawm and Ranger 1983).

Both adult education and community education have been referred to in this chapter as having traditional interpretations. In these cases, both concepts do have a lengthy history, and their traditions have a basis in historical practices. The point, however, is that, in recognizing and referring back to such traditions, we are really seeking to compare current practices with an idealized version of what once was. This is, of course, a source of further tension.

A third and final theme harks back to the discussion in the introduction of this chapter, and has to do with the relations between the various institutionalisations of adult education and training and those for child and youth education. These were expressed in terms of four dichotomies: compulsory/post-compulsory, initial/post-initial, secondary/post-secondary and school/post-school.

The existence of four such dichotomies is evidence enough of the problems in drawing a clear boundary between adult and non-adult education and training. Taken together, they indicate the existence of inevitable overlaps in institutional forms – most evident in England in further education colleges, in North America in community colleges. We might, therefore, conclude that any attempt neatly to delimit a field of adult education and training, the subject of this book, is doomed to failure. Or we might, more positively, argue that it is better to think in terms of an overarching concept such as lifelong education (see Chapter 2), encompassing all forms and levels of education throughout life.

FURTHER READING

Advisory Council for Adult and Continuing Education (1982) *Continuing Education: from policies to practice*. Leicester, ACACE.
    Well argued case for the development of an all-embracing system of continuing education.
Barnett, R (1990) *The Idea of Higher Education*. Buckingham, Open University Press.
    Thoughtful and carefully structured exploration of the meaning of higher education, though the language is at times rather difficult.
Coombs, P and Ahmed, M (1974) *Attacking Rural Poverty: how nonformal education can help*. Baltimore, Johns Hopkins University Press.
    Introduces the ideas of non-formal and informal education, and examines their application in the context of development.
Jarvis, P (1995) *Adult and Continuing Education: theory and practice*. London, Routledge, second edition.
    Standard text which contains a useful chapter analysing the various concepts discussed in this chapter.
Lovett, T (1982) *Adult Education, Community Development and the Working Class*. Nottingham, University of Nottingham Department of Adult Education, second edition.

Puts forward the case for an activist, involved and confrontational view of community education.

Martin, I (1987) 'Community education: towards a theoretical analysis', pp. 9–32 in, G Allen, J Bastiani, I Martin and K Richards (eds) *Community Education: an agenda for educational reform*. Milton Keynes, Open University Press.

The opening analytical chapter of a book which examines the status of community education from a variety of perspectives.

Rogers, A (1986) *Teaching Adults*. Milton Keynes, Open University Press.

Useful text, including a chapter which looks at the varied meanings of adult education and education for adults.

Chapter 4

Work-related concepts

EDUCATION AND THE ECONOMY

The concepts discussed in this chapter focus on the relationships between, on the one hand, adult education and training, and, on the other, labour market issues and economic growth (cf. the discussion of development in Chapter 1). The nature of these relationships, and their strength, weakness or absence, has been at the forefront of much recent debate on educational and training policy. Most educators, employers and politicians appear to believe implicitly that education, training and learning, broadly defined, can and should make a substantial, if perhaps indirect, contribution to economic production and growth (Hicks 1987). Indeed, many commentators use this belief to underpin their arguments for a greater investment by all concerned in education and training (Ball 1990; Finegold *et al.* 1990; Layard, *et al.* 1994; National Commission on Education 1993; Smithers and Robinson 1989).

The belief in a close and manageable linkage between education and the economy may been seen in operation on at least three levels; those of the individual, the organization and of the whole society:

- at the individual level, the participant in education, learning or training may regard this as a personal investment in their own future, during which some financial return may be expected;
- at the level of the organization, the belief takes the form of regarding expenditure on staff training and human resource development as an investment in the survival and development of the organization;

- at the level of the society, as represented through national policy, it supports the many measures which have been taken – in the United Kingdom through the Departments of Education and Employment (since 1995 linked in one department) – to encourage increased participation in further, higher and continuing education, and in vocational preparation, training and up-dating.

In conceptual terms, these beliefs find expression in the related notions of lifelong education, the learning organization and the learning society (discussed in Chapter 2). These concepts encapsulate the perceived need for all to engage in continuing and productive learning activities at individual, organizational and societal levels. They enjoy a broad acceptance, at least at the political or rhetorical level.

It is not surprising, therefore, to find many work-related concepts in common use in the field of adult education and training. The emphasis in this chapter is on concepts which deal with the relationship between education and the economy on a practical, rather than political, level. The four concepts selected for detailed discussion – human capital, human resource development, career, and professional – are, arguably, of particular prominence at this level. They allow for interpretations which emphasize the individual or the organization, and can accommodate both broader and narrower vocational perspectives.

HUMAN CAPITAL

The theory or concept of human capital was developed by economists from the 1960s onwards (Becker 1993; Schultz 1961, 1971; Woodhall 1987). Put simply, this theory encapsulates: 'the idea that people spend on themselves in diverse ways, not only for the sake of present enjoyments but also for the sake of future pecuniary and non-pecuniary returns' (Blaug 1992, p. 207).

While the theory has applications which go far beyond the relationship between economics and education:

In the field of education, the principal theoretical implication of the human capital research program is that the demand for postcompulsory education is responsive both to variations in the direct and indirect private costs of schooling and to variations in the earnings differentials associated with additional years of schooling.

(Blaug 1992, p. 208)

Distinctions may be drawn between general and specific human capital, with the former applying to 'skills and knowledge which enhances the worker's productivity, regardless of where she is employed', and the latter to 'skills which can be productively used only by the worker's current employer' (Johnes 1993, pp. 14–15). The clear implication is that the latter will be of most concern to the employer, who will tend to see it as wasteful to educate employees for potential employment elsewhere. General human capital development is seen as being chiefly the concern of the state or community, through its provision of general education and training.

At the aggregate, macro level, it is not difficult to produce evidence to suggest a monetary linkage between education and employment. For example: 'The difference in lifetime earnings between the average American who doesn't complete high school and the average American who completes college and continues to participate in some form of adult education is roughly $631,000' (Carnevale 1992, p. 60).

The survey data on which such broad conclusions are based may also be used in a more disaggregated form. It is then possible, with certain assumptions, to make detailed calculations of the rates of return – to the individual, to the organization, or to society – of a given investment in education or training, in terms of the discounted value of the probable future earnings of those concerned (Psacharopoulos 1987). Human capital theory argues that we do routinely make such calculations, though not usually in so much detail.

This notion of individual adults as rational economic decision-makers, assessing the possible returns to different personal investments in education, learning or training and then acting accordingly, has proved a very fruitful assumption for classical economists. It clearly does not, however, provide a complete explanation of adults' behaviour or participation in learning. Individuals do not act wholly rationally, whether judged in economic or other terms; and nor, of course, do organizations or governments. These realizations have led economists to develop alternative or supplementary theories to accompany or replace human capital theory (Chapman 1993). Two of these developments have been particularly influential.

First, what is called the 'screening hypothesis' suggests that one of the main qualities that employers look for in recruits, or candidates for promotion, is a certain level of education or training, usually measured by educational or professional qualifications. They may be satisfied with this quality alone – using qualifications as a 'signal' of the needed ability – or may want other qualities or skills in addition. Possible candidates are, therefore, screened for their educational qualifications, and those who pass this initial sifting exercise may either be employed directly or proceed to a second stage in the selection process. The implication of this view for the individual is that personal investment in education is only worthwhile up to the level required to enable them successfully to pass through the screening process for the job or career they are seeking. Beyond that, they would be better advised to invest in other things.

However, it is argued that: 'the weight of evidence suggests that signalling and screening account for only a small part of the differential between the earnings of relatively educated and less educated individuals' (Johnes 1993, p. 20). So it would seem that many employers may not screen, or at least do not screen in the rigorous fashion implied.

The second, and related, theory is that of credentialism. This suggests that, in an increasingly competitive labour market, those seeking employment or promotion will need to offer more and more qualifications if they are to stand out. The number, level and standard of qualifications required for a given post is seen as rising, regardless of their relevance (Dore 1976; Oxenham 1984). The implication for individuals is that they will need to invest more and more in their own education, training and development to keep up with, or stay ahead of, competing individuals:

> When students invest in their own 'human capital', as well as purchasing education in the form of a positional good they are often purchasing *savoir* [i.e. self transformation]. In the process of (as they hope) securing access to the labour markets, they are also turning themselves into more skilful and economically competent individuals.
>
> (Marginson 1995, p. 22)

In such a climate, most if not all investments are likely to be worthwhile.

The available empirical evidence on the relations between participation in education and training and employment does not wholly confirm or refute either human capital theory or its variants. That there is a linkage between education and the economy is rarely disputed, but the linkage is clearly neither direct nor simple. The notion that one might be able to predict, at either the individual or generational level, the likely future financial benefits of educational participation with a high degree of accuracy and confidence has yet to be realized. Such calculations are affected in complex ways by both individual characteristics, such as age, race and gender, and changing economic and social conditions.

Indeed, one of the authors quoted in this section, Blaug, judges that human capital theory has developed little in recent years, and sees no prospects for it doing so (Blaug 1992).

HUMAN RESOURCE DEVELOPMENT

Human resource development is, in origin, an American concept, the use of which was promoted in the UK by the Manpower Services Commission and its successor bodies. In these interpretations, the concept is seen as referring to a range of responsibilities and activities which have in the past tended to be located under headings such as 'personnel', 'staff development' or 'training'. It may also be seen as a more modern alternative to the notion of manpower planning, which now has a rather dated and sexist feel (Bartholomew 1976; Romiszowski; 1990).

In some other countries, however, such as the newly industrializing nations in East Asia, human resource development has a meaning closely analogous to that of development (discussed in Chapter 1). In such societies, the state is seen as having the core role in directing, focusing and coordinating policy and provision, rather than the individual firm or organization (Cummings 1995).

In its western interpretation, human resource development suggests a wide-ranging concern with the overall development of the individual, normally in their capacity as an employee or worker, and forms one aspect of the broader field of human resource management or planning (Harrison 1988, 1992; Molander and Winterton 1994). As in the case of many of the concepts discussed in this book, there is a range of definitions available:

> It should be no surprise . . . that because different disciplines lay claim to the field and emphasize different roles, each asserts a different definition of the field of practice. Each definition also implies an underlying philosophical stance regarding the nature of learning and instruction. Six characterizations capture the differing foci of these discipline-based definitions: human resource developer as competent performer, developer of human capital, toolmaker, adult educator, researcher/evaluator, and leader/change agent.
>
> (Watkins 1991, p. 242)

The competing disciplines identified include economics, adult education, psychology and management; while the writers associated with the six characterizations include, respectively, Mclagan, Carnevale, Jacobs, Nadler, Goldstein and Senge.

Nadler, one of the gurus of the field, portrays human resource development as: 'Organized learning, over a given period of time, to provide the possibility of performance change or general growth of the individual' (Nadler and Nadler 1990, p. xxvii).

For another group of authors, however, it is: 'The term used to describe an integrated and holistic approach to changing work-related behaviour, using a range of learning techniques and strategies' (Megginson et al. 1993, p. 10).

Watkins herself adopts the following definition: 'the field of study and practice responsible for the fostering of a long-term, work-related learning capacity at the individual, group and organizational level of organizations. As such, it includes – but is not limited to – training, career development and organizational development' (Watkins 1991, p. 253).

The first of these definitions, that provided by Nadler, appears at once to be so general that it could apply to any form of education or training anywhere, but also rather instrumental in its reference to performance change. The second definition is more restricted, explicitly focusing on work-related learning; but it appears more open in its reference to an integrated and holistic approach. Confining the field to 'changing', rather than say 'developing', work-related behaviour does, again, sound more instrumental. Thus, the final definition is perhaps the most satisfactory of the three, in suggesting the broad and critical role of human resource development within organizations and society.

As that definition suggests, human resource development is closely related to other concepts discussed in this book, including career (examined next in this chapter) and training (see Chapter 1). There is also a clear link with the idea of the learning organization, considered in Chapter 2. Learning organizations, if they merit the term, should see human resource development as a central and essential aspect of their activities.

All of these definitions leave somewhat unclear the question of what human resource development actually consists of, and, more specifically, just what it is that human resource developers do to be worthy of their rather impressive designation. Thomson and Mabey have, however, identified a lengthy list of tasks or roles, including:

- the recuitment and deployment of staff,
- the identification and improvement of employee skills and motivation,
- relating job content to organizational objectives and employee skills,
- reviewing the use of technology,
- performance management and measurement,
- identifying training needs,
- providing training and opportunities for self development,
- helping career management, and
- promoting change as both normal and an opportunity.

(Thomson and Mabey 1994, Chapter 1)

They see human resource development as a necessary, central and integrated response to a variety of contemporary pressures felt by organizations. These include competitive restructuring, decentralization, internationalization, organizational acquisitions and mergers, quality and service improvements (see the discussion of quality in Chapter 6), and technological changes (ibid.; cf. Mulder 1990).

There are, of course, objections to and criticisms of the idea of human resource development, and these can be found at both the conceptual and practical levels. In the former case, there are many who object to the idea of considering people as 'human resources', alongside and to some extent substitutable with non-human resources. This can seem to be both reductionist and demeaning, suggesting that individual adults are only to be considered in terms of their current and prospective future economic productivity. The idea of human resource development does, though, appear to represent an advance in these terms on the notion of manpower planning, in being somewhat less directive and more individualized. Perhaps we should talk instead, to use the title of a recent book, of 'developing resourceful humans' (Burton 1992)?

The practical objections to the concept are similar to those levelled at the ideas of human capital and the learning organization. Namely, just how many organizations or employers are currently using human resource development in anything like the central, integrated and comprehensive fashion suggested by the textbooks? While the pressures identified by Thomson and Mabey and other authors, referred to above, are undeniably potent, therefore, in the absence of a strategy based on human resource development, most organizations continue to respond in a piecemeal fashion.

CAREER

One of the roles of the human resource developer identified in the previous section was that of sharing responsibility for career management and development with the individuals concerned and their managers. This role would probably include the application of a range of techniques, such as career and performance reviews, mentoring, the use of psychometric and self-assessment tests, developmental assessment centres and career planning workshops, and the provision of information on alternative career paths (Mabey and Iles 1994). Indeed it has been argued that: 'In many ways career development and management succession planning are at the core of human resource development' (Thomson and Mabey 1994, p. 122).

Yet this is to suggest a rather narrow view of the meaning of career and career development; one which is, to some extent, supported by the inclusion of 'career' in a chapter entitled 'work-related concepts'.

There are a number of tensions apparent in studies of careers and career development. Thus, there are studies which focus on the individual level, and others which concentrate on careers within organizations (Kelly 1991; Sonnenfeld and Kotter 1982). Some researchers have seen careers essentially in terms of paid employment (e.g. Arthur *et al.* 1989; Brown 1984; Hall 1988; Watts 1981; Williams 1988), while others have taken a broader perspective, encompassing unpaid forms of work as well as overall life choices and circumstances (e.g. Hewitt 1993; Kerckhoff 1993; Super 1980).

The following is a well considered example of the former approach – equating the career with paid employment – to the study of individual or organizational careers:

> The term 'career' can mean a number of things. It can imply advancement – persons move 'up' in their career rather than 'down', although we refer to 'career moves', which may also be lateral. We also refer to people 'having a career in' some form of profession, such as medicine, banking or management, and there is an implication, if now largely out-of-date, that a career is likely to be stable over time. In fact it is becoming more common for people to think in terms of 'career portfolios', interrelated sets of work experiences that may be combined to provide career evidence for a range of jobs. Because of this, we shall define career as 'the pattern of work-related experiences that span the course of a person's life'. This definition not only broadens the concept of 'career', but makes it as relevant to unskilled and manual operators as to engineers and professors.
>
> (Thomson and Mabey 1994, p. 123)

This definition usefully brings out the class associations of the term. For some, however, its supposed breadth would be by no means broad enough:

> By career I mean that trajectory through life which each person undergoes, the activities he or she engages in to satisfy physical needs and wants and the even more important social needs and wants. The career, then, is activated in the service of both the physical being and the symbolic self.
>
> (Goldschmidt 1990, p. 107)

The first of these definitions can be characterised as narrower and vocational. It also focuses, at least implicitly, mainly on the experiences of men, given the emphasis on paid employment and continuity. The second definition, by contrast, is much wider.

It extends the notion of career both internally, in terms of its meaning for the individual concerned, and externally, linking work to the rest of life. As a concept, the latter is relevant to all, men and women, those in paid employment and those who are not.

Some, particularly older, studies of individuals' work careers have suggested that career development follows a regular pattern:

> career satisfaction follows a cyclical curve. It starts at a high level (upon occupational entry), dips to its nadir ... when initial expectations of rapid advancement are delayed or thwarted, and then recovers, although not to the previous high level ... at about age 40. In contrast, career success begins at a low ebb and increases linearly from occupational entry to midlife, when an incipient decline sets in.
>
> (Cytrynbaum and Crites 1989, pp. 68–9)

Such a view accords with many of the commonplace metaphors for work careers: the ladder, the set of steps, or the upward curve; followed by an inevitable but hopefully gentle slipping away in later life. Yet this pattern, though it undoubtedly has existed, and continues to exist, is by no means general and is rather simplified. It ignores the experiences of the many women who have 'career breaks', or who work in jobs with no development prospects, and is much less relevant in general at a time of recession and economic change. Hence, we may opt to speak instead of career patterns (Super 1980), career paths or career lines (Kerckhoff 1993).

These criticisms are confirmed by research which has focused on particular professions or areas of employment, such as teaching (Ball and Goodson 1985), medicine (Allen 1994) and management (Nicholson and West 1988). These studies have provided more comprehensive understandings of patterns of career development, and have challenged the more simplistic and unidirectional views of careers:

> Organisations are not pyramids, they are scattered encampments on a wide terrain of hills and valleys, and careers are not ladders, but stories about journeys and routes through and between these encampments.... Careers, as stories of these journeys, often get better with the telling....

They provide cognitive structures on to which our social identities can be anchored.

(Nicholson and West 1988, p. 94)

Other researchers have demonstrated the linkages between employment histories and life cycles (Kanchier and Unruh 1988), and shown that transitions at work and at home may be closely connected (Latack 1984). Individuals may adopt a range of different strategies to cope with the varying pressures of work and home, and thus balance and control their overall life careers (Dex 1991; Lambert 1990). They may seek to compartmentalize these roles, look for compensation in one area, for deficiencies in another, or allow the effects of one role to spill over into others (Blaxter and Tight 1994; Edwards 1993).

Studies of women's careers have contributed considerably to our understanding of the varied and broader patterns which careers may take. These studies have, naturally, paid particular attention to the conflicting demands of home, family and work (e.g. Brannen and Moss 1991; Evetts 1994; Gerson 1985; Hakim 1991; White *et al.* 1992). Mothers who seek to pursue or continue a work career necessarily have to make considerable compromises. They may have little alternative but to choose part-time or temporary employment. Their options are reinforced by processes of labour market segregation or segmentation, which effectively label work as women's or men's, and reserve certain types and levels of occupation, with poorer pay and conditions, largely or exclusively for women (Dex 1987; Rees 1992; Spencer and Taylor 1994).

A further challenge to the conventional view of the career has come from recent studies of the impact of changing economic and social conditions. For those starting careers, it is clear that the transition from initial full-time education to work has become problematic, and is likely to be smooth for only a minority of entrants (Banks *et al.* 1992). Recession, automation and changing employment patterns have led to increased youth and graduate unemployment, and to increases in part-time and short-term work. For those in work, organizational restructuring has considerably affected career expectations: 'The survivors of restructuring efforts are . . . well aware that while they may still have a *job*, they may no longer have a *career* – at least in the traditional ladder sense' (Kanter 1989, p. 308, original emphasis).

In these shifting circumstances, professional careers are be-coming less hierarchical but more entrepreneurial (Kelly 1991). The idea of the career portfolio or flexible career has been advocated, alongside that of the flexible firm or organization (Pollert 1991: cf. the discussion of flexible learning in chapter 5).

PROFESSIONAL

As in the case of the career, the linked ideas of 'profession' and 'professional' also have class and gender connotations, and have been the subject of some recent reappraisal. Unlike career and the other concepts discussed in this chapter, however, the term professional is not applicable to every individual adult, but is restricted to particular kinds of careers. It suggests both a certain, higher level of occupational activity and a degree of exclusivity. Like so many of the terms analysed in this book, profession presents problems of definition:

> *Profession* is an essentially contested concept. Despite its wide-spread use in the media and in the everyday discourse of those who would be readily regarded as professional people, and despite the best efforts of sociologists, philosophers and historians, it defies common agreement as to its mean-ing. Professions are more easily instanced than defined, and dictionaries tend to convey the meaning of the term more through example than by identifying distinctive qualities. Where qualities are cited these usually refer to *knowledge* and *responsibility*.
>
> (Hoyle and John 1995, p. 1, original emphasis: see the discussion of knowledge in Chapter 6)

Despite the authors' obvious reservations, the last sentence here brings across the idea of shared, learned values, frequently asso-ciated with the idea of a profession.

'Classic' professions such as medicine and law would likely be accepted as such by everybody. In most other cases, however, for example nursing, social work and school teaching, there would probably be disagreements as to status (Becher 1994). In such circumstances, it may be best to treat professionalism as an essentially ideological notion (Eraut 1994).

A variety of approaches have, nevertheless, been developed to summarize the characteristics, and enable the identification, of professions. These include the use of typical traits or sets of criteria, divisions of labour and occupational control (Jones and Joss 1995). Different forms of profession may also be recognized, such as the practical, technical and managerial, and, in addition, those termed reflective practitioners (Schön 1983, 1988). These forms may be distinguished in terms of their self-image, theoretical orientation, knowledge and value base, practice theory and client relations.

However, even if we do not have a shared idea of what constitutes a profession, it is still possible to discuss professional education, learning and training. Bines and Watson have identified three successive models of professional education:

> The first can be characterised as the 'apprenticeship' or 'pre-technocractic' model. Professional education takes place largely on the job.... The curriculum largely comprises the acquisition of 'cookbook' knowledge embodied in practice manuals and the mastery of practical routines. Instruction is largely provided by experienced practitioners.... The second model, called here the 'technocratic' model, has become the pattern of professional education for a large number of professions in recent years. It has tended to take place in schools associated with, or incorporated in, institutions of higher education. It is characterised by the division of professional education into three main elements ... the development and transmission of a systematic knowledge base ... the interpretation and application of the knowledge base to practice ... supervised practice in selected placements.
>
> (Bines and Watson 1992, pp. 14–15)

This quotation may be compared, in terms of its threefold historical typology, with that from Lessem on the development of management thinking in the section on the learning organization (see Chapter 2).

The third model identified by Bines and Watson 1992, the 'post-technocratic', is seen as still being in the process of development. It emphasizes the acquisition of professional competences through practice and reflection, with students having skilled practitioners as coaches or mentors. It may also be characterised by the increasing emphasis placed upon continuing professional development, accepting that professionals, like all workers, can no longer expect to be prepared for their whole careers during their initial education (Garry and Cowan 1986; Welsh and Woodward 1989).

LINKAGES AND INTERCONNECTIONS

The four work-related concepts discussed in this chapter have obvious interconnections. Thus, human resource development may be viewed as the process or processes by which human capital is developed. Similarly, the career, and its advancement, can, as already suggested, be seen as one of the key concerns of the human resource developer, and might also be thought of in terms of the application of individual human capital throughout the lifespan. Professions constitute a particular kind of career, and the role of human resource developer could itself be termed a profession.

These concepts do have a clearly work-related context, as do a number of others considered elsewhere in this book (see, for example, the sections on the learning organization in Chapter 2, and on skill, competence and quality in Chapter 6). However, they can also be interpreted more generally. This is particularly so in the case of career, where it has been argued that it is more useful to see the term as relating to the whole life rather than to just that component of it concerned with paid employment.

Taking this perspective, and interpreting the concepts discussed here, as indicated in the introduction, as operating primarily in practical rather than political terms, we can also view them as providing useful linkages between the levels of individual, organization and society. Each of the four concepts examined has individual and organizational elements, and each needs to be seen in the wider context of society as a whole. They deal with the development, productivity and output of individual adults as they impact upon the adults themselves, upon their employers or organizations, and upon the communities and nations of which they are a contributing part.

FURTHER READING

Arthur, M, Hall, D and Lawrence, B (eds) (1989) *Handbook of Career Theory*. Cambridge, Cambridge University Press.
    Collection of studies from a variety of disciplinary perspectives, but mostly focusing on career as paid work.
Blaug, M (1992) *The Methodology of Economics: or how economists explain*.

Cambridge, Cambridge University Press, second edition.
Accessible discussion of a wide range of economic theories, including human capital theory.

Eraut, M (1994) *Developing Professional Knowledge and Competence*. London, Falmer Press.
Focuses on the nature of professional knowledge, its development and assessment.

Harrison, R (1992) *Employee Development*. London, Institute of Personnel Management.
Standard how-to-do-it textbook including material on human resource development, career development and the learning organisation.

Johnes, G (1993) *The Economics of Education*. London, Macmillan.
General introduction to economic perspectives on education, including human capital theory and rate of return analysis.

Lambert, S (1990) 'Processes linking work and family: a critical review and research agenda'. *Human Relations*, 43, 3, pp. 239–57.
Useful literature review, summarizing a series of conclusions from the research analysed.

Thomson, R and Mabey, C (1994) *Developing Human Resources*. Oxford, Butterworth-Heinemann.
Another textbook with much material on human resource and career development practice.

Watkins, K (1991) 'Many voices: defining human resource development from different disciplines'. *Adult Education Quarterly*, 41, 4, pp. 241–55.
Review article which categorizes alternative views of human resource development.

Chapter 5

Learning concepts

THE ORGANIZATION AND PRACTICE OF ADULT LEARNING

This chapter considers a series of related concepts which are concerned with the methods by which adult education, training or learning are practised and organized. There is a plethora of such concepts, and new ones seem to be created (or recreated) every time a supposedly innovative learning initiative is launched.

For convenience, these 'learning' concepts can be divided into two main groups:

- those which focus mainly on the perspective of the organization providing education or training;
- those which are more concerned with the perspective of the individual learner.

It has to be recognized, of course, that this division is rather artifical, and that there are overlaps between the two groups.

The first group of concepts, emphasizing the organizational perspective, can be seen to include terms such as distance, flexible and open learning or education. There are, in addition, many other related, synonymous, cognate or precursor concepts – such as correspondence, external and 'non-traditional' provision – which belong with this group and merit some consideration.

The second group, stressing the individual learner's perspective, includes the closely linked concepts of experiential, independent and self-directed learning. Once again, there are a series of related terms which need to be borne in mind, including action, discovery, learner-managed and student-centred learning.

Two of the most widely discussed terms in adult education, andragogy and conscientization – ideas which have claims to be considered as the most, or perhaps only, original theories to be developed by adult educators – also belong in the second, individual group of learning concepts. They will be discussed separately, however, in recognition of their history and status.

What all of these concepts share in common, through their focus on the organization and practice of adult education and training, is a concern with issues of control and responsibility. Put simply, the concepts in the organizational group have to do with the ways in which those who provide education or training choose to offer these opportunities, with the control over the nature of this provision essentially retained by the institutions concerned.

In the case of the concepts included in the individual group, however, something of a shift of responsibility from the institution to the individual may be observed, with control over their learning resting to a larger, though by no means absolute, extent with the individual learner.

DISTANCE, OPEN AND FLEXIBLE

As suggested in the introduction, the three concepts on which this section will focus – distance, open and flexible learning, education or training – are selected, though arguably outstanding or at least representative, examples from a wider group. This broader group includes other terms which are precursors of, related to, or synonyms for, the three concepts chosen for more detailed exploration.

Thus, correspondence and external study may be seen as precursors of distance education, to be distinguished from it largely by the range and level of educational technologies used (Erdos 1967; Glatter et al. 1971; Houle 1974). Some now recognize a third 'generation' of practice in this area, developed from distance education and characterized by the use of computer-based instruction (Mason and Kaye 1989).

As a concept, distance education has itself now been partly superseded by the term open learning. However, the latter, like flexible learning, has a broader meaning as well, and could be seen as encompassing all of the concepts included in this chapter, in both the organizational and individual groups (Wedemeyer 1981).

The organizational group of concepts can also be seen to extend out to include overlapping, but narrower or less universal, terms such as extra-mural, non-traditional and part-time. There are also links between this group and ideas such as access and modularization, which are considered here with other 'structural' concepts in Chapter 7. The boundaries between conceptual groupings such as these are, evidently, difficult to draw, and the particular relationships discussed here should not be seen as hard and fast.

These problems of association may be further illustrated with reference to the terms programmed and discovery learning; both of which might have been considered in some detail in this chapter, but were judged to be of lesser significance. Thus, programmed learning now seems a dated and directive concept, yet was once thought, at least by some authorities, to hold great promise. Discovery learning, on the other hand, sounds a relatively timeless and idealistic notion. Yet both terms can be linked to generally desirable sounding ideas like open, flexible, independent and self-directed, and to each other, through the concepts of distance education and experiential learning.

Distance

The last two decades have witnessed an international upsurge of research in distance education, largely stimulated by the creation of the British Open University (Perry 1976) and of similar institutions in other countries. This research has included both comparative analyses of alternative systems (e.g. Kaye and Rumble 1981, 1991; Rumble 1986; Rumble and Harry 1982) and theoretical developments (e.g. Evans and Nation 1992; Perraton 1987). A number of authors, notably Bååth, Garrison, Holmberg, Keegan, Moore and Peters, have attempted to define distance education and suggest areas for further study within this field.

Thus Holmberg has built on the notion of distance education as a guided didactic conversation:

Distance education comprises one-way traffic by means of printed, broadcast and/or recorded presentations of learning matter and two-way traffic between students and their supporting organization. The one-way presentation of learning matter occurs either through self-contained courses or through study guides to prescribed or recommended reading. Most of the two-way traffic usually occurs in writing, on the telephone or by other media and, usually only secondarily or as a supplement, face to face.

(Holmberg 1986, p. 2)

This seems to be a very precise definition, but it is also restrictive. It appears to be based firmly on the contemporary practices of a limited number of institutions, including the British Open University and similar specialist institutions in other countries.

Keegan, on the other hand, starts his analysis from an explicit recognition of the range of different concepts and practices which have been drawn together under the banner of distance education:

'Distance education' is a generic term that includes the range of teaching/learning strategies referred to as 'correspondence education' or 'correspondence study' at further education level in the United Kingdom; as 'home study' at further education level and 'independent study' at higher educational level in the United States; as 'external studies' in Australia; and as 'distance teaching' or 'teaching at a distance' by the Open University of the United Kingdom. In French it is referred to as 'télé-enseignement'; 'Fernstudium/Fernunterricht' in German'; 'educación a distancia' in Spanish and 'teleducacão' in Portuguese.

(Keegan 1986, p. 31)

He then defines distance education in terms of five characteristics:

– the quasi-permanent separation of teacher and learner throughout the length of the learning process; this distinguishes it from face-to-face education.
– the influence of an educational organization both in the planning and preparation of learning materials and in the provision of student support services; this distinguishes it from private study and teach-yourself programmes.
– the use of technical media; print, audio, video or computer, to unite teacher and learner and carry the content of the course.

– the provision of two-way communication so that the student may benefit from or even initiate dialogue; this distinguishes it from other uses of technology in education.
– the quasi-permanent absence of the learning group throughout the length of the learning process so that people are usually taught as individuals and not in groups, with the possibility of occasional meetings for both didactic and socialisation purposes.

(Keegan 1986, p. 49)

Keegan also adds two 'socio-cultural determinants' which he regards as 'both necessary pre-conditions and necessary consequences of distance education'. These are:

– the presence of more industrialised features than in conventional oral education.
– the privatisation of institutional learning.

(Keegan 1986, p. 50)

Keegan's definition is more comprehensive than Holmberg's and it has been the subject of widespread discussion, criticism and amendment (e.g. Bååth 1981; Keegan 1989). Some have criticized Keegan's adoption of Peters' ideas regarding distance education as an industrialized form of education (Garrison and Shale 1990; Peters 1983); and/or the more modern version which portrays distance education as a Fordist form of production (Raggatt 1993; Rumble 1995). Some have seen distance education as involving a more general reconstruction of the time–space relations linking educational institutions and learners (Evans and Nation 1992). Others have sought instead to identify within distance education key dimensions such as communication, dialogue, structure, autonomy, independence and control (Moore 1990).

However, it may be more realistic and pragmatic to regard distance education as simply 'education at a distance' (Garrison 1989: just as adult education may be interpreted as 'education for adults' – see Chapter 3). That is, distance education may be viewed as just one form of education, sharing the same key characteristics as all other forms:

All of what constitutes the process of education when teacher and student are able to meet face-to-face also constitutes the process of education when teacher and student are physically separated. All the necessary conditions for the educational

process are inherent in face-to-face contact. They are not necessarily actualised, but the potential is always there. This is not
the case when teacher and student are physically apart. The
task of distance education is to find means by which to intro-
duce these necessary conditions, or to simulate them so closely
as to be acceptable proxies.

(Shale 1990, p. 334)

Perhaps the most telling criticism of the great majority of the
definitions of distance education that have been offered is their
idealization and unreality. There are few, if any, examples of institutions or courses which would meet in full the definitions of
either Holmberg or Keegan. Thus, it does not seem realistic to
imply, as in the first characteristic specified by Keegan, that
teacher/learner separation throughout the length of the learning
process is to be regarded as the norm in distance education.
Some elements or stages in the educational process (i.e. needs
assessment, programme planning, implementation, evaluation)
may be carried out at a distance, others face-to-face, others by
a mixture of these means. Indeed, in some institutions, both
distance and face-to-face forms of provision may be offered, with
a great deal of interchange and convergence in practice (Smith
and Kelly 1987).

Similarly, the second of Keegan's characteristics seems to over-
play, as does Holmberg's definition, the role and influence of
educational organizations. This might in many cases be confined
to particular, but perhaps critical, stages. Elements of private or
independent study may also be incorporated within or alongside distance study.

In the case of the third and fourth characteristics identified by
Keegan, further reservations are also called for. After all, the
technical media and two-way communication employed in
distance education may in practice be minimal, and possibly
absent entirely.

The more flexible conception which these criticisms imply
suggests that in reality there is a continuous spectrum between
face-to-face and distance forms of education (cf. the discussion
of the education/learning and education/training spectra in
Chapter 1). The ends of this spectrum are never encountered in
practice, while along it there are no absolute dividing lines (Tight
1987).

Many providers of distance education include elements, sometimes optional, sometimes compulsory, of face-to-face tuition within their programmes (e.g. Open University tutorials and summer schools). These may play a crucial role in the educational process. Perhaps more significantly, all providers of distance education – in common with all providers of face-to-face education – expect their students to engage in varying amounts of private or independent study on their own and away from the direct influence of the teacher or the course text.

Distance education, practically defined, might then be seen as a form of education in which distance teaching techniques predominate, but not to the exclusion of other methods (Kaye 1988; Shale and Garrison 1990; Verduin and Clark 1991). Such a definition would usefully set the particular approach of distance education within the more general context of open learning.

Open

The practice of 'openness' – the adoption of measures to encourage widespread access to and participation in education, training and learning – by universities, schools and other educational institutions is, contrary to received wisdom, of long standing (Bell and Tight 1993; Nyberg 1975). Yet, the encapsulation of these practices in a general philosophy of 'open learning' appears to be a relatively recent development (Bosworth 1991; Tait 1993; Thorpe and Grugeon 1987). It has been linked to the development of equal opportunities (Gilham 1995). It is also, like distance education, the subject of fierce debate (see, for example, Boot and Hodgson 1987; Rumble 1989).

Of the many definitions of 'open learning' which have been put forward during the last decade, the following two are not untypical:

> 'Open learning' is a term used to describe courses flexibly designed to meet individual requirements. It is often applied to provision which tries to remove barriers that prevent attendances at more traditional courses, but it also suggests a learner-centred philosophy. Open-learning courses may be offered in a learning centre of some kind or most of the activity

may be carried out away from such a centre (e.g. at home). In nearly every case specially prepared or adapted materials are necessary.

(Lewis and Spencer 1986, pp. 9–10)

Open learning is merely one of the most recent manifestations of a gradual trend towards the democratisation of education. The use of the term 'open' admits that education and learning have traditionally been 'closed' by various barriers – entrance requirements, time constraints, financial demands, geographical distances, and, much more subtly, social and cultural barriers, as well as those of gender. An open learning institution is one dedicated to helping individuals overcome these barriers to their further education.

(Paul 1990, p. 42)

Both of the authors quoted fall into the trap of seeing the practice, as distinct from the nomenclature, of open learning as a recent development, to be contrasted favourably with a 'traditional' and 'closed' approach (see the discussion of tensions, traditions and dichotomies in Chapter 3). This is both a gross simplification and a myth. The notions of openness and democratization have been practised in education since at least the time of ancient Greece, and possibly ever since education as such existed. Lewis's definition may also be faulted for putting too much emphasis on specially prepared materials, which need not be seen as essential.

Both definitions characterize open learning as being about the removal of barriers. These barriers can be classified broadly into three groups:

1   physical/temporal: those restricting the time, place and pace at which learning may be undertaken;
2   individual/social: those to do with the characteristics of individual learners (e.g. age, sex, ethnicity, class, wealth);
3   learning: those to do with the nature of the learning provided (e.g. content, structure, delivery, accreditation, flexibility).

By implication and contrast, open educational or training institutions are in the business not just of removing some or all of these barriers, but of going further to adopt positive, outgoing and involving attitudes, practices and images to the community at large.

It would be foolish, of course, to imagine that any one educational institution or provider could realistically attempt to be wholly open in all of these ways. Most of those who see themselves as being involved in open learning have focused their openness on a particular group or set of characteristics, and remain relatively 'closed' in other ways (Harris 1987).

This has not prevented a proliferation of programmes and institutions with the word 'open' in their titles (Bagley and Challis 1985; Birch and Latcham 1984; Scottish Education Department 1982). In the United Kingdom, the national Open College, various regional Open Colleges or Open College Federations and Networks, the Open Learning Foundation, the Open Polytechnic and the Open Tech – some of them longer lasting than others – have all followed the lead of the Open University.

The naming of the British Open University itself led to an understandable confusion between the two terms 'distance education' and 'open learning', which some have taken as virtually synonymous. But the messages conveyed through the word 'open' are clearly just too good to miss:

> Open learning is an imprecise phrase to which a range of meanings can be, and is, attached. It eludes definition. But as an inscription to be carried in procession on a banner, gathering adherents and enthusiasms, it has great potential. For its very imprecision enables it to accommodate many different ideas and aims.
>
> (Mackenzie *et al.* 1975, p. 15)

Most worrying, perhaps, is the use of open learning to refer to the use of learning packages designed to impart work-related skills cheaply and with minimal support (McNay 1988). In the 1980s, open learning, in this narrow sense, was increasingly adopted in the UK by both industry and government as a cost-effective substitute for more conventional forms of training: 'ideas originating in the quite different context of opening up access for adults to higher education have been imported into training for teenagers in work-related skills' (Bynner 1992, p. 105).

In reality – as in the case of distance, face-to-face and private education – we should probably view all educational providers as operating somewhere along a spectrum between 'openness' and 'closure'. Their position on this continuum can be judged by their attitude to the who, why, what, how, where and when questions of study (Lewis 1986).

Flexible

The use of the term 'flexible learning' – as opposed to 'open learning', to which it can be seen as analogous – is closely associated in the United Kingdom with the further education sector. Its development is particularly linked to the work of the Further Education Unit (FEU). The concept has been simply defined by the FEU as: 'the adaptation of available learning opportunities to meet the needs of the learner in a way that optimises the autonomy of the learner as well as the effectiveness of the process of learning' (FEU 1983, p. 11).

The FEU has also identified a series of dimensions of practice along which the degree of flexibility practised by an educational or training provider may be judged. These include the aims and content of learning, the characteristics and stage of development of the learner on entry, the mode of learning, the resources available for training, mode of attendance, pace of learning, interactions with others and methods of assessment (FEU 1984). These dimensions have similarities with those identified by Lewis for open learning.

The idea of flexible learning, like open learning, has received the backing of the British government, and been incorporated in various government funded initiatives designed to develop skills in the labour force (Department of Employment 1991; Tomlinson and Kilner 1990). It has also become subsumed within the later idea of the 'responsive college' (Theodossin 1986), a term for describing institutions which are flexible or open to the needs of their students and clients (cf. the 'flexible organization': Pollert 1991). Most recently, it has been increasingly applied in higher education (Thomas 1995; Wade *et al.* 1994).

One influential example of the application of the idea of flexible learning in practice, which has clear connections with both distance and open learning, was the development of 'flexistudy' by the National Extension College (NEC) and its partners during the late 1970s (NEC 1981; Sacks 1980). Flexistudy is in essence a mixed mode form of provision, embodying varied elements of distance and face-to-face education. The NEC's role was to produce the distance elements: packages of course materials to support study in a range of subjects and at a variety of levels. These materials would then be used in dual settings; both by the individual student when studying alone at home or at work, and by them when they made occasional visits to their local college for tutorials or group sessions.

The students involved are recruited by the colleges, not by the NEC. They can be recruited at any time of the year, and allowed to learn at their own pace. With the course materials being produced nationally, minority subjects can be accommodated. Flexistudy suited both the colleges and the NEC. The colleges were provided with a flexible mechanism, and with high quality materials, for supporting a wide range of local study needs. The NEC was removed from the administrative chores of direct national recruitment and was able to give effective local support to students (Freeman 1982).

EXPERIENTIAL, INDEPENDENT AND SELF-DIRECTED

The second group of learning concepts to be considered in this chapter differs from the first in focusing more on the perspective of the individual learner than on that of the organization providing the learning opportunities. As already suggested, however, this distinction is by no means clear cut.

Three concepts will be considered in some detail in this section: experiential learning, and the closely linked notions of independent and self-directed learning. As with the organizational group, there are a number of other related concepts in common use. These include action and discovery learning, which are most closely related to the concept of experiential learning; and autonomous, individualized, learner-managed, resource-based and student-centred learning, which have close affinities with the ideas of independent and self-directed learning (e.g. Graves 1993; Long 1990).

Two further learning concepts with a particular focus on the individual learner – andragogy and conscientization – are then considered in the following section. These may be distinguished from experiential, independent and self-directed learning in terms of their status and centrality within adult education thinking over the last three decades.

Experiential

A number of different uses of the concept of experiential learning are current. One recent study identified four main interpretations, emphasizing the role of experiential learning as:

- the assessment and accreditation of learning from life and work experience;
- a means of bringing about changes in the structures, purposes and curricula of post-school education;
- a basis for group consciousness raising, community action and social change; or
- a means for increasing self awareness and group effectiveness (Weil and McGill 1989).

These interpretations were then associated with the work of particular authors, including, respectively, Evans, Kolb, Freire (see the later discussion of conscientization in this chapter) and Rogers.

Kolb's work on the theoretical foundations of experiential learning can be seen to underlie most, if not all, approaches in this area. It has also been influential in developing our broader understanding of the nature of learning (see section on learning in Chapter 1). Kolb builds on Lewin's four-stage feedback model of learning, which involves concrete experience, observation and reflection, the formation of abstract concepts and generalizations, and the testing of the implications of these in new situations. Consequently, he defines learning as: 'the process whereby knowledge is created through the transformation of experience' (Kolb 1984, p. 38). This simple model of learning has been very influential amongst adult educators and trainers (e.g. Boud *et al.* 1993 Burnard 1988).

Its influence can be seen, for example, in the movement to allow the accreditation or assessment of prior learning, or of prior experiential learning (abbreviated as APL, APEL and various similar acronyms: see also accreditation in Chapter 7). This movement has achieved particular prominence during the last decade, having been imported into the UK and other countries from the USA. It starts from the recognition or assumption that many adults possess considerable knowledge, understanding or skills, often developed through work, social or voluntary activities, which has not been, but is worthy of, accreditation towards an appropriate qualification (Evans 1992). Evans has defined the concept as follows:

> Experiential Learning means the knowledge and skills acquired through life and work experience and study which are not formally attested through any educational or professional certification. ... Hence the assessment of prior experiential learning (APEL) refers to all learning which has not been assessed. This marks it off from the assessment of prior learning (APL), which also includes learning which has been assessed for some formal purpose.
>
> (Evans 1994, p. 1)

The various methods involved in producing and assessing evidence of prior learning are now widely understood and accepted. However, their implementation remains patchy. While APL and APEL have made inroads into further education, where they are seen as one more means of developing flexibility, they have yet to be so widely accepted in higher education (Challis 1993; Field 1993; Simosko 1991).

The third and fourth interpretations of experiential learning identified by Weil and McGill are particularly associated with more 'traditional' or radical forms of adult education (see the discussion of adult and continuing in Chapter 3). The former interpretation would typically seek to embody a recognition of the value of each individual adult's experience, and then endeavour to use and build upon it in the learning experience. The latter would include, for example, initiatives with women's, black or working-class groups (e.g. Fordham *et al.* 1979).

But other uses of the term 'experiential learning' are also current. Thus, for example, experiential learning has been defined as: 'synonymous with "meaningful-discovery" learning. ... This is learning which involves the learner in sorting things out for himself [sic], by restructuring his perceptions of what is happening' (Boydell 1976, p. 19). In this form the concept has been linked with both autonomous, integrative and action learning (McGill and Beaty 1992; Revans 1982). It has become influential within management development thinking (Kolb *et al.* 1986), and has contributed to the creation of the idea of the learning organization (see Chapter 2).

Independent and self-directed

These two concepts are so closely linked that they will be treated here as essentially synonymous. They have obvious connections with the practice of distance education, discussed earlier in this chapter. In distance education, the learner and teacher are normally separated in both space and time, so that the distant learner is also to a greater extent independent or self-directed (Henderson and Nathenson 1984; Moore 1983).

However, like open learning, these concepts have a broader association as well. That is, they refer to all cases where the responsibility for, and control of, the learning experience – its planning, delivery and assessment – is largely transferred from the institution to the individual learner.

The idea of self-directed learning is particularly associated with the work of Tough, who carried out or inspired a body of empirical research in the 1970s and 1980s (Tough 1971, 1976, 1989; see also, for example, Brookfield 1981, 1982; Penland 1979). Tough believed that much significant learning was carried out by individual adults in the form of learning projects, largely outside of the influence of formal educational institutions (cf. informal learning, discussed in Chapter 3). He defined a learning project as a 'highly deliberate effort to gain and retain certain knowledge or skill', and set an arbitrary minimum length of seven hours.

From his studies, Tough estimated that the average or median adult conducted 8 learning projects lasting 700 hours in total in a year. Of these, two-thirds were planned by the learner, and only one-fifth by a professional educator. The most common motivation for learning was some anticipated use or application of knowledge or skill, with less than 1 per cent of projects being undertaken for credit.

The research of Tough and his associates has been influential, but has also been criticized. These criticisms include the focus of most of the studies on middle-class respondents, the tendency to reduce their experiences to quantitative measures rather than exploring the quality of the learning engaged in, the concentration on the individual as opposed to their broader social context, and the lack of attention given to the implications of the research findings (Brookfield 1984). More recent studies have, therefore, looked at how adult educators might best act as facilitators for

those engaged in self-directed learning, and at how these practices might be built into educational programmes (e.g. Boud and
Higgs 1993).

A leading British example of supported self-directed or independent study is that provided by the University of East London
(formerly the North East London Polytechnic). Here methods
were developed to enable individual students to study for qualifications independently, with the support of specialist staff,
group sessions and the facilities of the institution. These
processes had to meet the criteria and standards set by the
accrediting body; initially the Council for National Academic
Awards (CNAA), later the institution itself. The individual
student is responsible for determining their own curriculum,
syllabus, study methods and assessment pattern, for getting
these approved, and for scheduling and carrying out the work
involved. In other words, the student and the institution draw
up a learning agreement or contract.

The programme led initially to the Diploma in Higher
Education (DipHE), but was then extended to enable a whole
first degree to be completed by independent study (O'Reilly 1991;
Percy *et al.* 1980; Stephenson 1980). Though the quality of the
support offered has been subject to some criticism, the
programme continues to offer a relatively open route to and
through higher education for mature students. Many of these
students come from educational and social backgrounds not
normally associated with such study, and might not have
engaged in higher education at all had this opportunity not been
available.

Building on similar practices in a range of institutions, a
number of researchers have attempted to articulate theoretical
models of self-directed learning. Their work has linked the
concept with ideas such as critical reflection and internalized
'learning conversations'; as well as, inevitably, experiential learning (Boud *et al.* 1985; Candy *et al.* 1985). Thus, two
of these researchers, for example, have defined the concept of
self-directed learning in the following way: 'Self-organization
consists in the ability to converse with oneself about one's
own learning processes and to observe, search, analyse, formu-
late, review, judge, decide and act on the basis of such
creative encounters' (Thomas and Harri-Augstein 1985, pp.
xxvii–xxviii).

Few adults will, of course, be in a position to do this unaided. The purpose of adult education and training then becomes, in large part, the development of such abilities in the individual learner.

ANDRAGOGY AND CONSCIENTIZATION

The two concepts discussed in this section share a number of characteristics in common. They both came to prominence in the English-speaking world in the 1960s and 1970s. They both derived from non-western sources: andragogy stemming from Eastern Europe and conscientization from Brazil. They both made their chief proponents – Malcolm Knowles in the case of andragogy and Paulo Freire in the case of conscientization – famous, at least within the world of adult education and training.

However, while it would be difficult to ignore these concepts in a book of this nature, they may both now be seen as somewhat dated and out of fashion. When they were first articulated in the west, they had a radical feel to them. This has now either become compromised or has been overridden by more pragmatic interests.

Andragogy

The concept of andragogy – whether seen as a theory, a set of hypotheses or just as guidelines for practice – has been the subject of extensive discussion over the last two decades:

> This concept is the single most popular idea in the education and training of adults, in part because and for the way in which it grants to educators of adults a sense of their distinct professional identity.
>
> (Brookfield 1986, p. 91)

Though the term originates from Europe (Krajnc 1989), it owes its later development and popularity to the work of an American adult educator, Malcolm Knowles (Knowles 1970, 1973, 1985). He defined andragogy, in contra-distinction to pedagogy, rather loosely as 'the art and science of helping adults learn'. While Knowles' interpretation and application of the concept have varied somewhat over the years, a series of assumptions about individual adult learning have remained at the core:

As a person matures:
(1) his [sic] self-concept moves from one of being a dependent personality toward one of being a self-directed human being;
(2) he accumulates a growing reservoir of experience that becomes an increasing resource for learning;
(3) his readiness to learn becomes oriented increasingly to the developmental tasks of his social roles; and
(4) his time perspective changes from one of postponed application of knowledge to immediacy of application, and accordingly his orientation toward learning shifts from one of subject-centredness to one of problem-centredness.

(Knowles 1970, quoted in Tight 1983, p. 55)

Knowles then goes on to identify 'conditions of learning' for adults, together with associated 'principles of teaching'.

While Knowles' arguments for andragogy have met with considerable enthusiasm and support on both sides of the Atlantic (e.g. Allman 1983; Mezirow 1981), they have also been the subject of much criticism (e.g. Brookfield 1986; Martin 1986; Tennant 1988). These critiques have tackled the underlying assumptions of andragogy one by one. Thus, the widespread existence of self-direction amongst adults (see the previous section), and its implied absence in children, has been queried. Similarly, the problem-centred focus of adult, as opposed to child, learning has been questioned. The third assumption has been seen as ignoring the reflective, personal and serendipitous aspects of adult learning, and of suggesting a reductionist and behaviouristic, competency-based approach to practice (see the discussion of competence in Chapter 6).

Of the four assumptions, it is the second which has been least criticized: 'it is this second assumption of andragogy that can arguably lay claim to be viewed as being a "given" in the literature of adult learning' (Brookfield 1986, p. 98). Yet, even in this case, the significance of the assumption for adult education and training practice has been doubted: 'experience may well be a characteristic that sets children apart from adults, but it is not a characteristic which is relevant in distinguishing between good educational practice for adults and good educational practice for children' (Tennant 1988, p. 21).

After such a barrage of criticism, there may seem to be little left for the concept:

> Given the semantical problems in Knowles's definition of andragogy, the lack of clarity and specificity in his underlying assumptions, the research reports which do not support and sometimes even refute it, and the mounting academic criticism of it as a legitimate theory or approach, one might ask if andragogy retains any utility or viability for the discipline of adult education.
>
> (Davenport 1987, p. 19)

Yet that author still saw a role for andragogy, suitably refined and redefined, recognizing the public relations value of the concept. There seems to have been less discussion of andragogy in adult education and training circles over the last few years. It can reasonably be concluded that any aspirations for presenting andragogy as an overarching theory are now gone, though it retains some value as a guide to practice, and remains popular in some areas.

Conscientization

The term conscientization is closely associated with the work of Paulo Freire, a Brazilian adult educator who has achieved worldwide renown. The work through which Freire developed his conceptual ideas was carried out in the poorer areas of Recifé, in North East Brazil, and had a particular focus on developing the literacy of men. It extended far beyond the inculcation of basic skills, however, to concern itself with broader themes of individual emancipation. Given these concerns, it is not surprising that Freire ran into political opposition, and spent many years in exile in other countries.

Freire's work and writing is probably the best example in the field of adult education and training of ideas from the developing world coming to have a major influence in the industrialized world. It raises the issue of whether such cultural transfers are either practical or useful, not just at the intellectual level but also in terms of practice, as Freire's methods have been adopted and adapted with mixed success in many countries (e.g. Kirkwood and Kirkwood 1989; Mackie 1980; McLaren and Lankshear 1994). More specifically, since Freire wrote in

Portuguese, and has been read by most people in translation, it may be that much has been lost in that process.

Thus, Freire himself has always used the Portuguese term 'conscientização' rather than the most obvious or convenient English translation, 'conscientization', which is repeated here. His two most influential books, both now over twenty years old, define this term in the following, somewhat divergent but complementary, ways:

> Conscientização is the deepening of the attitude of awareness characteristic of all emergence. . . . In contrast with the antidialogical and non-communicative 'deposits' of the banking method of education, the programme content of the problem-posing method – dialogical par excellence – is constituted and organized by the student's view of the world, where their own generative themes are found.
>
> (Freire 1972, p. 101)

> Conscientização represents the *development* of the awakening of critical awareness. It will not appear as a natural byproduct of even major economic changes, but must grow out of a critical educational effort based on favourable historical conditions.
>
> (Freire 1974, p. 19, original emphasis)

The concept is articulated in opposition to what Freire calls the 'banking' method of education; in other words, the notion that students' minds are 'empty vessels' to be filled up by the wisdom and expertise of their teachers. For Freire, true education or learning is about dialogue, and is about giving the student space and support to develop their ideas and themselves within, and against the background of, their social, political and economic context.

For others, the real power of this idea lies not just in the process itself, but in the transformation it may bring about in the learner: 'Conscientization is a process of developing consciousness, but consciousness that is understood to have the power to transform reality' (Taylor 1993, p. 52).

Clearly, there are many linkages between Freire's idea of *conscientização* and other contemporary educational concepts. Freire himself makes the link with critical consciousness, and others have made a connection with consciousness raising, with its particular associations in the 1970s in the west with the women's movement (Mezirow 1981). The related notion of education as being about individual and collective emancipation or empowerment have also already been mentioned, though linking conscientization with enlightenment may be going too far (Matthews 1980).

The linkages are, however, much broader than this:

> The idea of analysing one's experiences to achieve liberation from psychological expression or social and political oppression is a recurring theme in adult education. It is most commonly associated with the work of Freire, but it is also a feature of some contemporary conceptions of self-directed learning, andragogy, action research, models of the learning process and techniques of facilitation.
>
> (Tennant 1988, p. 140)

This effectively associates Freire with some of the most widely regarded western adult educators, including Knowles and Tough. It also makes Freire's position apparent in the debate about the respective roles of teacher and learner (see the sections on learning and teaching in Chapter 1).

Like Freire, both Knowles and Tough came to prominence a few decades ago. Though their place in the adult education 'Hall of Fame' seems assured, their ideas about the curriculum have been supplanted in the political consciousness by other concepts. These concepts – such as capability, enterprise, competence and quality (all discussed in Chapter 6) – have a harder and more pragmatic ring to them. Set against them, conscientization seems in some ways to be even more radical than it was in the 1960s.

CONCEPTUAL COMPETITION

All of the concepts discussed in this chapter are clearly related to each other. Whether their major focus is on the institutional provider of learning opportunities, or on the individual learner, they all present idealizations of how adult learning and training might best be delivered. It might reasonably be questioned, therefore, why there appear to be so many competing concepts in this area.

A number of possible, and no doubt partial, explanations suggest themselves. First, we are here dealing with groups of concepts which have been advanced over a period of decades, and which have come to prominence in different countries. Second, we have to recognize the breadth and looseness of the field of adult education and training. There may be relatively little communication between, for example, those concerned with management development and those leading literacy and basic skills groups in deprived communities. In these circumstances, there may seem little to wonder at in the existence of a whole range of closely related concepts.

Yet these reasons do not wholly or satisfactorily explain the persistence of so many overlapping ideas. To do so, we need to add an appreciation of the politics of the field we are studying. Put simply, the organizations and individuals that develop and promote particular learning concepts will have put a lot of work and commitment into them, and are unlikely to be willing to see them subsumed into more generally accepted terms without considerable resistance.

FURTHER READING

Brookfield, S (1986) *Understanding and Facilitating Adult Learning*. San Francisco, Jossey-Bass.
    Includes a thorough review and critique of the concepts of andragogy and self-directed learning.
Evans, N (1994) *Experiential Learning for All*. London, Routledge.
    Another book by the leading British proponent of the accreditation of prior experiential learning.
Further Education Unit (1983) *Flexible Learning Opportunities*. London, Further Education Unit.
    A straightforward outline of the concept as seen by its leading proponent, and of its application to English further education.
Garrison, D (1989) *Understanding Distance Education: a framework for the future*. London, Routledge.
    One of the most accessible accounts of this field, which is sensibly modest in the claims that it makes.
Kolb, D (1984) *Experiential Learning: experience as the source of learning and development*. Englewood Cliffs, Prentice Hall.
    Standard work by the leading theoretician of experiential learning.
Lewis, R and Spencer, D (1986) *What is Open Learning?* London, Council for Educational Technology.
    One of a series of texts on the subject published by the CET, this one focuses on the meaning and types of open learning.
Tait, A (ed.) (1993) *Key Issues in Open Learning: a reader. An anthology from the journal 'Open Learning'*, 1986–1992. Harlow, Longman.

A selection of articles from the journal based at the British Open University: not surprisingly, a lot of the papers chosen focus on distance education, and on the Open University in particular.

Weil, S and McGill, I (eds) (1989) *Making Sense of Experiential Learning: diversity in theory and practice*. Milton Keynes, Open University Press.
A thoughtful study of different interpretations of the term, arguing for the need to understand and share different perspectives.

Chapter 6

Curricular concepts

DEVELOPING THE CURRICULUM

Curriculum development, which is concerned with the aims, processes and outcomes of educational provision, has become an area of increasing importance within adult education and training over the last few decades (Squires 1987, 1990). Two main, linked reasons for this may be identified: the overall rise in levels of provision and participation, and the increased interest taken by the government and other external authorities in the nature of the education and training being delivered. What is taught, and how it is taught, are currently seen as being issues of more general concern, and not to be left to individual teachers, their employers or institutions.

As in the case of many of the other areas considered in this book, there is an extensive range of concepts in use, of which only some will be analysed here. The term 'curriculum' is itself, of course, a concept of note. It is one which has been extensively discussed from a school-based perspective, while accorded relatively little attention by adult educators (Griffin 1983). There are a number of tensions evident within these discussions between differing views of the curriculum:

- curriculum as an area of study (i.e. a syllabus) or all of an educational institution's activities;
- curriculum as content, product or process;
- the formal, informal and hidden elements of the curriculum (Kelly 1989).

The approach taken in this chapter will be both broad, in its interpretation of the scope of the curriculum, and selective, in its choice of concepts for examination. The emphasis will be on overall approaches to the curriculum, rather than particular aspects of its planning, delivery or evaluation. The chapter starts with what may be seen as the more 'traditional' concepts of knowledge and skill. These concepts can be seen to underpin all adult education and training, as well as embodying some of the opposition (see the section 'vocational or liberal?' in Chapter 1) evident between education and training.

The remainder of the chapter will then focus on four concepts which have a very different feel to them. Though by no means new, they have come into, or back into, prominence during the last few years. These concepts are those of competence, capability, enterprise and quality. They share the characteristic of resulting largely from the intervention within education and training of outside interests.

KNOWLEDGE AND SKILL

The concepts of knowledge and skill have a long history and a widespread common usage. As already suggested, they can be seen as representative of the perceived dichotomy between education and training. They are not, of course, the only such oppositional terms. With a little thought, a list can readily be compiled (see Figure 6.1). To take this presentation a little further, the latter of each pair can be seen as useful, general, external and to do with the 'real' world, while the former may be caricatured as useless, élitist, internal and within the ivory tower. Such caricatures are only such of course, and fall down as soon as any more detailed analysis is engaged in. Yet, they do have purchase and influence, and are not so far away from being the views of many of those with power to influence education and training.

education	versus	**training**
knowledge	versus	**skill**
understanding	versus	**experience**
theory	versus	**practice**
academic	versus	**vocational**

Figure 6.1 Conceptual dichotomies

What, then, is meant by 'knowledge'? One prominent writer on adult education has come up with a useful observation: 'Knowledge may be seen as a level of awareness, consciousness or familiarity gained by experience, learning or thinking' (Jarvis 1983, p. 66). This formulation has the advantage of being applicable to all, while allowing for the existence of a variety of, potentially conflicting, knowledges.

More absolutist and objective conceptions of knowledge are still, of course, adhered to by many, particularly those coming from a background in the pure sciences. Others, including the present author, lean towards more relativistic and changing perceptions. This is not to deny the power of science, however, or its general view of its subject matter as potentially entirely knowable, but to recognize that such an approach does not work from all disciplinary perspectives. Sociologists, for example, will typically see knowledge, like truth, as socially constructed (Blackledge and Hunt 1985). Many philosophers, similarly, see it as inseparably connected with power:

> Knowledge, therefore, does not simply represent the truth of what is but, rather, constitutes what is taken to be true. . . . Thus, rather than taking changes in knowledge as the progressive unfolding of truth, it is necessary to examine the complex exercise of power which is immanent in such changes.
>
> (Usher and Edwards 1994, pp. 87–8)

Within educational circles, there are also debates about whether knowledge, as opposed to a concept such as understanding, is an aim of education or training (Barrow and Milburn 1990: see also the section on education in Chapter 1). After all, knowledge, in everyday speech, has associations with quiz shows, memorization feats and superficiality. In this sense, its opposite or antithesis is ignorance rather than skill.

In some ways, therefore, it may be more helpful to think in terms of types of knowledge. Thus, we might distinguish between empirical, formal and philosophical knowledge; or propositional, skill and acquaintance knowledge. Bloom and his colleagues, in a widely cited but probably less well read study, identified six main categories of educational objectives in the cognitive domain: knowledge itself (defined as recall), comprehension, application, analysis, synthesis and evaluation. These make the connection between knowing, in its everyday sense, and understanding (Bloom 1956). Learning theorists, such as Gagné, similarly recognize a hierarchy of levels of learning (Gagné 1985: see also the section on learning in Chapter 1).

It is also possible to differentiate between general knowledge and the wide range of special knowledges shared by particular groups of people. Eraut, for example, in a study of managers, has identified six types of knowledge: situational, people, practice, conceptual, process and control. These, he claims, may be generally applicable, at least to other professions (Eraut 1990, 1994).

When we begin to compartmentalize knowledge in this way, we get somewhat closer to the notion of skill. Here, again, there are problems with different disciplinary definitions and interests:

> Labour economists generally see skill as a property of an individual, made up of various combinations of education, training and competence. Industrial sociologists, on the other hand, have normally regarded skill as an aspect of jobs themselves, derived from the imperatives of industrial and technological organisation, without giving much attention to the relations between the skill of jobs and the skill of people. . . . Social historians have focused predominantly on the skilled divide within the manual working class and particularly on the role of apprenticed craftsmen in the development of trade unionism. There is, therefore, no shared conception of skill amongst social scientists. The concept is both multivalent and complex.
>
> (Francis and Penn 1994, p. 223)

Yet, while recognizing these differences, we can go further than this. One analyst, for example, working from a comparison of the professional and amateur approaches to painting a room, has identified five main characteristics of skill: fluency, rapidity, automaticity, simultaneity and knowledge (Sloboda 1986). Given the context of the present discussion, the last of these may seem particularly interesting.

Another author presents a somewhat similar listing:

> There are four criteria for the application of the term 'skill':
> 1. A situation of some complexity.
> 2. A performance that addresses the situation, is deliberate and is not just a matter of chance.

3. An assessment that the performance has met the demands of the situation.

4. A sense that the performance was commendable.

(Barnett 1994, p. 56)

This formulation does not specify, but implies, the existence of some relevant knowledge.

From these analyses we can detect some of the problems with applying the concept. For it is not just multi-valent but multi-level: we can use the same term to talk about an international concert pianist and our local plumber. Not surprisingly, it is with the latter that most concerns are raised: namely, how to increase the skill levels of the broad mass of the working population in order to enable us better to compete in the global economy.

This interest, coupled with the recognition that neither education nor work is for life, has led to the recent concern with developing what have been called personal transferable skills (Bradshaw 1992; Bridges 1993; Silver 1988). Developed in the initial period of education, and refined through continuing education and training, such generic skills are supposed to make workers more flexible, adaptable and able to learn. Personal transferable skills are at the heart of the capability and enterprise initiatives, discussed in the next section, and are also central to the competency movement, the subject of the section after that.

Before leaving the concept of skill, however, we should recognize that, like knowledge and other concepts, it is both socially constructed and a political term. The degree to which a performance is regarded as commendable, to use Barnett's words, is a matter of perception, and that perception crucially depends upon status: the status accorded to the performer and the performance, and the status of the person making the judgement. Hence, the concert pianist is likely to be regarded by most people as more skilful than the local plumber.

Since issues of power and status are involved, skill also has a crucial gender component:

The classification of women's jobs as unskilled and men's jobs as skilled or semi-skilled frequently bears little relation to the actual amount of training or ability required for them. Skill definitions are saturated with sexual bias.

(Phillips and Taylor 1986, p. 55)

These views are linked to perceptions of paid and unpaid work, and to the varied interpretations of career (Sinclair 1991; see the section on career in Chapter 4). There are clear implications here for changing patterns of work: 'Feminisation of a particular occupation or profession is seen to have the effect of deskilling it' (Rees 1992, p. 17). School-teaching, for example, particularly at primary level, might be seen as an illustrative case of this process in operation.

CAPABILITY AND ENTERPRISE

Capability and enterprise are both concepts which came into prominence in the United Kingdom in the 1980s. They do, however, have a longer history and more general meanings, and have also been similarly applied in the last few years to education and training in other countries (e.g. Bennett and McCoshan 1993; Shuttleworth 1993).

While there are similarities between these two concepts, there have been key differences in their promotion and in the level of resourcing behind them. Capability was a slogan launched by the Royal Society of Arts, a body concerned to bring together educators and industrialists and to advance their joint interests. Enterprise, on the other hand, was one of the key concepts underlying the thinking of the Conservative governments of the period, and heavily funded through the Manpower Services Commission and its successor bodies (Barnett 1994; Burgess 1986). It was a characteristic of both of these initiatives that neither of the promoting bodies saw a pressing need to define what they were talking about, or seeking to encourage, with any precision. It was left, at least initially, to those seeking funding or support through the initiatives to interpret or second guess what the promoters were after. This was sometimes excused on the grounds of the difficulty of definition:

> Capability does not lend itself to detailed definition. It is easier to recognize it than to measure it with any precision. It is an integration of confidence in one's knowledge, skills, self-esteem and values. . . . Capable people have confidence in their ability to (1) take effective and appropriate action, (2) explain what they are about, (3) live and work effectively with others, and (4) continue to learn from their experiences, both

as individuals and in association with others, in a diverse and changing society.

(Stephenson 1992, pp. 1–2)

As this quotation indicates, however, the early reluctance to be precise was soon supplanted by a quite detailed, though not necessarily particularly helpful, formulation. What is given here is a very general definition of some of the desirable qualities of fellow workers or citizens. There are not many hints as to what a 'capability curriculum' might look like, nor as to how it might differ from learning activities lacking that conceptual heading.

This lack of precision did not, however, prevent a broad mixture of educators and industrialists from endorsing the Education for Capability movement. Nor did it stop the officers of that movement from visiting and recognizing courses or programmes as developing capability in their students.

Not surprisingly, these processes themselves led to the identification of some common features. Thus, the leaders of the Higher Education for Capability offshoot of the movement came to recognize four themes:

● reviewing and building upon previous experience, knowledge and skills;
● preparing plans and negotiating approvals;
● active and interactive learning;
● the assessment of performance according to agreed learning outcomes (Stephenson and Weil 1992).

The enterprise initiative, or initiatives, may be seen to be more narrowly focused than the capability movement. Its concern was with the development of just work, rather than work and life, skills.

The Conservative governments of the 1980s were responsible for launching and funding a whole raft of enterprise schemes. These covered the themes of employment and unemployment, and education and training. They ranged in their targets across the lifespan from schoolchildren through youths to older adults. Among the schemes were, for example, the Technical and Vocational Education Initiative, the Enterprise Allowance Scheme, Enterprise in Higher Education, Enterprise Awareness in Teacher Education and even Evangelical Enterprise (MacDonald and Coffield 1991).

Enterprise in Higher Education (EHE), to take just one example, was launched in 1987, and promised one million pounds each to higher education institutions which were prepared to embed enterprise throughout their curricula. As in the case of the capability movement, enterprise was not initially defined (Burke 1991), but it was clearly implicit that only applications endorsing the Manpower Services Commission's particular view of enterprise would receive funding. Within a year of the launch, the sponsors, now renamed as the Training Agency, had become more explicit:

> As well as being qualified in a particular discipline, students who have attended a course which includes enterprise will:
> – have a positive attitude towards enterprise activity;
> – have developed personal transferable enterprise skills;
> – be better informed about employment opportunities, aims and challenges and make better career choices;
> – be better prepared to contribute to and to take responsibility in their professional and working lives.
>
> (Training Agency 1989, p. 5)

Tensions can be identified within this statement between the development of 'skills' and the inculcation of 'attitudes' (as they similarly can be in the reference to values in the capability definition quoted). Some have seen this as tantamount to suggesting a process of indoctrination to make students more favourably disposed towards enterprise. The vocational focus is transparently obvious. Most EHE programmes duly involved local employers in the planning, delivery and even assessment of courses, and developed 'realistic' project work and placement schemes. Bids for funding identified a limited range of personal transferable skills which would be developed in students, typically including problem-solving, groupwork and presentational skills.

With a further year's experience of the programme, the Training Agency was ready to reflect back to its educational audience the implicit and explicit meanings of the concept which they had identified:

> There are many definitions of 'enterprise'. Definitions may focus on:
> ● Entrepreneurship: the qualities and skills which enable people to succeed in business enterprises

• Personal effectiveness: the qualities and skills possessed by the resourceful individual
• Transferable skills: the generic capabilities which allow people to succeed in a wide range of different tasks and jobs.

(Training Agency 1990, p. 5)

A reasoned assessment of the Enterprise in Higher Education initiative would be that it has had modest success, in terms of getting academics to think about and implement both curriculum and staff development (Becher 1994; Her Majesty's Inspectors 1992). However, both the concept and its implementation have been heavily criticized. For some this critique has been based on what is seen as unwarranted government interference, for others on a challenge to the traditions of liberal education, and for still others on the perceived inability of employers to make effective use of recruits with enterprise skills (Bailey 1992; Foreman-Peck 1993; Tasker and Packham 1994).

More generally, the whole 1980s movement for embedding industrial values within education, of which the capability and enterprise schemes can be seen as parts, has been ably deconstructed by Coffield:

> We are not dealing with a tightly defined, agreed and unitary concept but with a 'farrago' of hurrah words like 'creativity', 'initiative' and 'leadership' . . . some notions which are central to most definitions of enterprise, problem-solving for instance, have been taken from psychology and then simplified, decontextualised and invested with a significance and power which few psychologists would be prepared to support . . . the potential terms of reference of words like 'capability' or 'skills' (or 'enterprise') are so wide that to call someone 'capable' or 'skilful' (or 'enterprising') without specific context is meaningless . . . enterprise tends to be viewed as an individual attribute and both structural factors and local economic conditions are ignored . . . where is the independent and convincing evidence of the success of enterprise education or enteprise initiatives?

(Coffield 1990, pp. 67–8)

The problem with capability and enterprise is not just that they are so self-evidently (in these applications) transient buzz-words, lacking in hard, analytical credibility; but in the assumptions which they make about educators and trainers, their employers and their clients. These groups are seen simultaneously as sharing common aims and being highly malleable. That the commonality of their aims might be only apparent at a general and simplistic level, disguising an underlying and possibly healthy diversity of practice, is not seen as important, provided that they can be persuaded or cajoled into endorsing and operating common approaches.

The capability and enterprise movements may thus be seen as expressions of a fundamental lack of trust in British education and training institutions and providers. The drive towards competency-based education and training, the subject of the next section, may be viewed in a similar fashion, though it differs in terms of both its overall scope and the degree of control imposed. In that sense, it represents a further development of the desire to centralize influence and control over a recalcitrant educational service.

COMPETENCE

Like many educational developments, the examples for the introduction of competency-based education and training in Britain have been drawn from North America; in this case building on the practices of scientific management and functional analysis. The spur for their application, however, has been the perceived lack of relevance of existing vocational provision and the need to compete better with other economies:

> One of the growing concerns amongst employers has been that much of the provision of VET [vocational education and training] was not seen as being directly relevant to the needs of employment ... it was considered that VET tended to be 'educationally' oriented both in content and the values which are implicit in its delivery. It has tended to concentrate on the acquisition of knowledge and theory while neglecting performance, and it is performance which essentially characterizes competence.
>
> (Jessup 1989, p. 66)

In response, the British government set up a Working Party on Vocational Qualifications, which reported in 1986. It defined its core interests in the following terms:

A vocational qualification is a statement of competence clearly relevant to work and intended to facilitate entry into, or progression in, employment, further education and training, issued by a recognized body to an individual. This statement of competence should incorporate the assessment of:
- skills to specified standards;
- relevant knowledge and understanding;
- the ability to use skills and to apply knowledge and understanding to the performance of relevant tasks.

(Working Group on Vocational Qualifications 1986, p. 17)

Competence itself was defined later on in the report as 'the ability to perform a particular activity to a prescribed standard' (ibid., p. 59). This framework was quickly accepted by the government of the day, and a National Council for Vocational Qualifications (NCVQ) was established to oversee the rapid introduction of National Vocational Qualifications (NVQs) throughout education and training (Burke 1989, 1995; Hodkinson and Issitt 1995; Jessup 1991).

The introduction of a national competence-based education and training (CBET) system was welcomed in some quarters as providing a positive challenge:

CBET has a constructive effect on some long-held assumptions about designing and assessing learning programmes. ... It confronts the unthinking acceptance of institution-bound, formal, time-served programmes, and raises questions about whether traditional forms of assessment really do address the learning outcomes teachers claim to promote.

(Ecclestone 1994, pp. 155–6)

However, the introduction of a new model for vocational education and training, on the basis of little research or piloting, was not without its problems. Much initial effort was devoted to the identification of what competences actually measured and what they did not:

Competence is concerned with what people can do rather than with what they know. This has several implications:
firstly if competence is concerned with doing then it must have a context . . .;
secondly competence is an outcome: it describes what someone

can do. It does not describe the learning process which the individual has undergone . . .;

thirdly in order to measure reliably someone's ability to do something, there must be clearly defined and widely accessible *standards* through which performance is measured and accredited;

fourthly competence is a measure of what someone can do *at a particular point in time.*

(Unit for the Development of Adult Continuing Education
1989, p. 6, original emphasis)

Others stressed the use of criterion-referencing, whereby the individual's performance is measured against some constant scale (e.g. Wolf 1995). Most conventional educational programmes, by contrast, tend to employ norm-referencing, which relates the individual's performance to that of their fellow students.

The development of a competency-based system in the United Kingdom required, and still requires, a great deal of thought, analysis, staff development and paperwork (Bees and Swords 1990; Fletcher 1991; Lloyd and Cook 1993). It also fairly immediately involved the practitioner in a consideration of what UDACE referred to as 'context', and what the Working Party itself described as 'relevant knowledge and understanding', linked to the competences under consideration.

Hence it became necessary to identify not only the specific competences required and tested for, but also what became known as their 'underpinning' knowledge and understanding. When this was taken into account, the idea of competence could be talked of in rather broader terms:

This is a wide concept which embodies the ability to transfer skills and knowledge to new situations within the occupational area. It encompasses organisation and planning of work, innovation and coping with non-routine activities and includes those qualities of personal effectiveness required in the workplace to deal with co-workers, managers and customers. It also encompasses the idea of being able to perform these different tasks over a period of time.

(Debling and Hallmark 1990, p. 9)

Such a description seems little removed from the concepts of capability and enterprise, discussed in the preceding section.

The British government's policy for the introduction of competency-based education and training is far from being completely implemented. Not surprisingly, it has attracted a good deal of criticism, though perhaps not as much as might have been expected. British educators are, to a considerable degree, punch-drunk and demoralized after many years of rapid policy change, and hence less able to, and interested in, resisting than they might otherwise have been. One of the earlier published critiques noted that:

> The idea of assessing through the use of competence statements and associated performance criteria is superficially attractive since it appears to guarantee a certain level of ability which may be expected to be transferable from the specific situation in which it was acquired. However ... the competence notion has been stretched too far ... we believe that 'competence' is the embodiment of a mechanistic, technically-oriented way of thinking which is normally inappropriate to the description of human action, or the facilitation of the training of human beings.
>
> (Ashworth and Saxton 1990, pp. 23–4)

Others have attacked the policy as imprecise, confused, reductionist and applicable only to certain lower level skills or activities: 'These aims are basic minimum, lowest common denominator ones, and leave just about everything else to be said about VET, adult and higher education' (Hyland 1994, p. 99). These criticisms suggest a linkage between the concept of competence and the notion of professionalism (Eraut 1994: see the section 'professional' in Chapter 4), which may be seen as being beyond 'mere' competence. They also raise the issue of the connection between competence and expertise; particularly as the competence movement has been seen by some as being about deskilling as much as reskilling, and about the assertion or reassertion of control by the state over certain professions, such as teaching (Jones and Moore 1993).

In contrast to the more general term 'competence', both professionalism and expertise may be interpreted as having to do with higher level skills. It is in this sense that we may distinguish between the concert pianist and the local plumber, already referred to in the section on 'skill' above. For there are some activities or events which require more than mere competence.

The link between competence and expertise is made explicit in the Dreyfus model of skill acquisition, which recognizes five successive stages: novice, advanced beginner, competent, proficient and expert (Dreyfus *et al.* 1986). The distinction between these two concepts is spelt out in Benner's application of the Dreyfus model to nursing:

> Competence, typified by the nurse who has been on the job in the same or similar situations two to three years, develops when the nurse begins to see his or her actions in terms of long-range goals or plans of which he or she is consciously aware. . . . The expert performer no longer relies on an analytic principle (rule, guideline, maxim) to connect his or her understanding of the situation to an appropriate action.
>
> (Benner 1984, pp. 25–6, 31)

In other words, experts can perceive large and meaningful patterns in their domains of expertise, and they have deeper levels of understanding (Glaser and Chi 1988).

QUALITY

The current focus on the quality of education and training provision in the United Kingdom has, to some extent, paralleled the introduction of competency-based systems, though the former concern is much more international in its scope (Craft 1994; Freedman 1987; Vroeijenstijn 1995). It can be seen as impacting upon all levels of provision, from school through further education and university to professional and continuing education (e.g. Ashworth and Harvey 1994; Doherty 1994a; Ellis 1993; Holloway 1994; Tovey 1994; Zuber-Skerritt and Ryan 1994). The emphasis, however, has been primarily upon formal providers of education and training.

The initial reaction to the late 1980s quality debate from professional educators and trainers, and their employing institutions, can probably best be characterized as one of scepticism. With strong governmental support, and given the state's position as the major funder of most educational institutions, such scepticism was, however, of little avail. The model for quality which was adopted was that of the successful private company, and so the mechanisms for ensuring quality in education and training were largely taken, with little adaptation, from manufacturing industry:

> We now have a plethora of custodians of quality, all of whom are at least to some extent legitimated by the Education Reform Act of 1988, the Further and Higher Education Act of 1992 as well as the White Paper with its concerns for quality and accountability. The latter, particularly, not only referred to levels of quality assurance: quality control, validation and examination, and external assessment, but also specifically mentioned quality systems – BS5750 and Total Quality Management (TQM).
>
> (Doherty 1994b, p. 3)

In addition to quality assurance, control, validation, examination and assessment, reference may also be found to quality audit, management, enhancement, circles and improvement teams (see also the discussion of human resource development in Chapter 4). As well as the British Standard BS 5750, there is an International Standard ISO 9000; and, within the United Kingdom, there are related schemes such as Investors in People and the Management Charter Initiative (Critten 1993). These techniques and standards are being applied throughout the public, private and voluntary sectors, and not just in the areas of education and training (see, for example, Morgan and Murgatroyd 1994).

It would not be far-fetched to say that, in a very short space of time, a minor quality industry has grown up within British education and training. It is an industry with competing branches, and one which is placing an increasing bureaucratic load on those responsible for the actual delivery of education and training.

Amid all of this activity, however, relatively little attention has been given to just what might be meant by quality, and to whether it has distinct characteristics in an educational context. It is, after all, commonplace to hear and read statements along the lines of 'I don't know what quality is, but I know it when I see it' (cf. the quote from Stephenson in the section on capability earlier in this chapter). After all, quality, like standards, is a concept or principle with which it is very difficult to disagree (Williams 1988).

While this does not excuse us from our task, it is as well to recognize the difficulties and the resonances attached to words like 'quality':

> Quality, like 'freedom' or 'justice', is an elusive concept. We all have an instinctive understanding of what it means but it is difficult to articulate. Quality is also a value-laden term: it is subjectively associated with that which is good and worthwhile.
>
> (Green 1994, p. 12)

It is also a contested concept which embodies tensions within itself. Thus, in the idea of quality assessment, we can identify tensions between:

- the demands of external accountability and the processes of internal improvement;
- the idea of a gold standard and of something that is 'merely' fit for its purpose;
- criterion and norm referencing (i.e. do we judge quality in terms of some absolute standard or with reference to our competitors?);
- assessment of inputs and/or outputs, or of the whole educational or training process;
- cross-disciplinary or discipline-specific demands;
- responsive or strategic approaches (see Barnett *et al.* 1994).

It is difficult to see, of course, how anyone could ever be entirely satisfied with the quality of anything, be it an artifact or a service. We could always potentially do better. So there is no end to quality assurance and assessment. Seen in this light, the current concern with quality may, in reality – like the capability, enterprise and competence movements – be in large part to do with control: 'the truth is that QA [quality assurance] is a grandiose term for any well-run management system' (Freeman 1993, p. 14).

A POLITICAL BATTLEGROUND

A series of common themes can be recognized running through the discussion of the six terms which have formed the focus for this chapter. These themes can be seen in operation at a number of levels.

Thus, we can identify tensions within the concepts themselves. If we call someone skilful, capable, enterprising or competent, are we saying something banal or praiseworthy? Are these minimal or acceptable standards? How can they be measured or assessed? This tension can even be detected, though to a lesser extent, in the concepts of knowledge and quality. If, for example, we refer to something as everyday knowledge, we may, depending upon our perspective, be dismissing it as commonplace or holding it up as of value.

Second, the interrelationships between the concepts analysed are close and complex, involving opposition and overlap. It is common to find advocates of one concept decrying another, reflecting the continuing dissonance between the core concepts of education and training. Yet it is also common to see the concepts identified defined in terms of, as well as in relation to, each other. The closer the analysis, the more skill slides into knowledge, and the nearer competence comes to understanding.

Third, this conceptual battleground is also, and perhaps primarily, a political battleground. Underlying the debates reviewed here is a fundamental challenge to the professionalism of educators, trainers and their institutions. This challenge is coming from policy-makers and funders who are convinced that, in this case, the British vocational education and training system has not been delivering what is required of it, to the detriment of the competitiveness of the economy. Hence we are not just dealing with concepts here, but also with slogans and their supporting ideologies.

FURTHER READING

Barnett, R (1994) *The Limits of Competence: knowledge, higher education and society.* Buckingham, Open University Press.
    Careful unpacking of many of the conceptual issues surrounding the use of the terms 'knowledge' and 'competence', with particular reference to higher education.
Coffield, F (1990) 'From the decade of enterprise culture to the decade of TECs'. *British Journal of Education and Work,* 4, 1, pp. 59–78.
    Comprehensive discussion and critique of the British Conservative governments' education and training policies during the 1980s.
Doherty, G (ed.) (1994) *Developing Quality Systems in Education.* London, Routledge.
    Useful accounts of the impact of the quality debate at different educational levels.

Squires, G (1987) *The Curriculum Beyond School*. London, Hodder and Stoughton.
  General discussion of curricular issues in adult, further and higher education.

Chapter 7

Structural concepts

INPUT, EXPERIENCE AND OUTPUT

This chapter examines a series of concepts which have to do with the structure, volume and experience of adult education and training. Collectively, these concepts are concerned with a group of important issues:

- inclusion within, and exclusion from, provision;
- how what is offered is organized; and
- what benefits and disbenefits (or 'costs) stem from participation.

In other words, the content and the ordering of the discussion in this chapter can be seen to parallel the processes of education, learning and training themselves; moving from input through experience to output.

Clearly, there are linkages between this chapter and the preceding two, which are concerned with learning and curricular concepts. While this chapter focuses on the overall organization of the learning experience, Chapter 5, on learning concepts, looks at some of the models which have been applied to adult education and training. Chapter 6, on curricular concepts, examines some of the issues or ideas which have been seen to underlie approaches to education and learning. As this synopsis itself indicates, however, the distinctions between the kinds of concepts discussed in these three chapters are relatively fine ones, and they could, of course, have been organized rather differently.

The six concepts analysed in this chapter have been grouped in three pairs: access and participation, accreditation and modularization, and success and dropout. The first pair have to do with entry to the learning experience, both at the individual level and in overall terms. The second two are concerned with different ways of organizing or recognizing the learning experience to which entry has been gained or granted. The third pair relate to the results of the learning experience, and how these may be assessed or evaluated.

ACCESS AND PARTICIPATION

Access and participation are now among the major policy issues in post-school education, both in the United Kingdom (see, for example, Fulton 1989; Parry and Wake 1990; Smithers and Robinson 1989) and worldwide (Bélanger 1991; Davies 1995; Halsey 1992). Not surprisingly, as with most policy developments, this interest and concern has what might be seen as positive and negative aspects. Thus, on the one hand, there are those who are primarily concerned with opening up study opportunities for both more and different people. Then, on the other hand, there are the fears which have been created by the fluctuations and decline in the size of the conventional further and higher education entry cohort: the 16–19 year olds. A common response to these trends has been the increased recruitment of adults into formal education, which itself has given rise to concerns about falling standards or 'more being worse'.

While the concept of access has undeniable political resonances, whether the subject is access to education, healthcare, social security or whatever, the idea of participation may seem to be more neutral and thus straightforward. The individual adult is either a participant – engaging in education, learning, training or whatever activity is of interest (Smith *et al.* 1980) – or a non-participant. This status may change from time to time, but at any one point should be clear. In practice, however, participation may not be so clear-cut, not only because of the rather amorphous nature of activities such as learning, but also because the extent of individual commitment may vary. Thus, participation can be viewed as a continuous rather than a dichotomous variable (Cookson 1986).

The problematic nature of the concept becomes more apparent when possible definitions are considered. The Organization for Economic Cooperation and Development (OECD), for example, once defined participation, in the context of adult education and training, in the following terms: 'to qualify as a participant an adult should attend a sequence of meetings or complete a cycle of exercises' (OECD 1977, p. 11). This is the kind of definition which is used by institutional providers and those responsible for the collection of statistical information or the disbursement of funds. Yet, it immediately raises a whole series of practical and detailed questions. How many meetings? How many exercises? Does the learner have to be present throughout the meeting, and be active while present, to qualify as a participant? Do they have successfully to complete exercises?

These questions are not trivial. They underlie many of the methodologies which funding bodies use to determine the allocation of resources to educational institutions. They also necessitate a good deal of time-consuming and bureaucratic activity in order to produce satisfactory responses. The quality of these responses will, of course, as with any human activity, be variable, partly because of the quality and precision of the definitions on which they are based.

Given these reservations, we should be careful in interpreting statistics on participation in adult education and training. Yet a considerable amount of research in this area has focused on the collection of data, through surveys of adult participation (and non-participation) in education and training at national, local or institutional level. Much effort has also been expended upon attempts to explain the data collected, and the patterns found in or suggested by them.

Participation surveys typically involve the administration of a large number of questionnaires or structured interviews to a selected sample or defined group of the general adult population at a specific time (e.g. Gallie and White 1993; Sargant 1991; Training Agency 1989). They are thus cross-sectional in nature. Longitudinal studies, which trace adults' participation over a period of time, are much less common (e.g. Banks *et al.* 1992; Jenson *et al.* 1991).

Such surveys normally collect information on a wide variety of individual characteristics which might affect participation or non-participation in education and training, including social, economic and demographic factors. They may also record details of any educational or training courses which their respondents are following, and of other learning activities which they are engaged in. The large quantitative data sets which result from these surveys then readily lend themselves to cross-tabulation or correlation exercises, as well as to more complex multivariate analyses.

Participation surveys provide the major source of data for understanding why adults involve themselves in learning, the routes they take through education and training, their experience along the way, and the effects which this has upon them (Courtney 1992; Cross 1981; Maguire et al. 1993; McGivney 1990). They typically show, for example, a strong relationship between adult participation and previous educational experience and qualifications, and varied linkages between the kinds of learning activities engaged in and the sex and age of the participant (Tight 1995).

To date, however, such studies have not led to the development of a comprehensive and successful theory which can be used to explain why adults engage in learning activities, and how this relates to their work and other roles. To gain this kind of understanding, more detailed, more narrowly focused, longitudinal and qualitative methods of research would seem to be required.

The concept of access is, as already mentioned, avowedly political. It can be seen as offering one means for analysing the broad question of participation. Access has to do with who gets educational or training opportunities and who does not. This interest operates at both the individual level and in overall terms, when gender, class, wealth, 'race', disability and other social characteristics may be seen as of key importance. Thus, participation surveys consistently demonstrate that access to higher status forms of education and training is granted disproportionately to white, middle-class and able-bodied men.

Adult education may in itself be seen as expressing an ideology of needs, access and provision (Griffin 1983). In other words, it has, and has always had, an essential concern with issues of access. In the British context, however, and in many other industrialized countries, the impact of the idea of access has arguably been felt most keenly during the last decade or so, and then in the sectors of, first, higher education and, more recently, further education and training.

The remainder of this section will consider the example of higher education in a little more detail. In this case, access has been articulated by recent governments as one means of influencing the profiles and practices of higher education institutions (Connelly 1991; Council for National Academic Awards 1989).

There is an important distinction to be drawn here, yet one that is often overlooked, between the broad idea of access and the much more specific manifestation of access courses. Access courses may be defined as those designed for mature students seeking entry to further or higher education, which offer an alternative to established examination systems designed for adolescents. While they have been of increasing importance, they are far from being the only methods of enabling adult access to further and higher education.

Those within the access course movement may be seen as working in a long-established tradition, sharing many of the beliefs and practices of some older forms of adult education (see the section on adult and continuing in Chapter 3). Their concern is chiefly with extending educational participation to those who would otherwise be excluded:

> The proponents of access courses themselves seem almost universally to belong to the *social engineering* approach to admissions. It is a radical movement in the sense that it sees education as a means by which whole social groups can improve their social, economic and political positions within British society. It is also radical in an educational sense. The social groups which represent the primary clients of Access courses are seen to have been 'failed' by the conventional educational system. The Access-course movement is founded on a rejection of such failure and of the criteria which have defined it.
>
> (Brennan 1989, p. 57, original emphasis)

The nationwide development of access courses to provide a 'third route' (alongside the existing routes through academic and vocational qualifications) into higher education offers a rather standardized solution to this perceived problem. While it is undeniable that they have enabled many individuals to pursue their education further than they might otherwise have been able to do, access courses arguably have yet to have a major impact upon the social make-up or assumptions of higher education (Halsey 1993; Halsey *et al.* 1980).

Access courses may also be criticized on a variety of other grounds (Tight 1993):

- they are often unnecessary, since many of their participants are already well qualified;
- they are often over-elaborate and too long;
- they help to create and sustain ghettos, labelling their participants as 'access course' students;
- they overemphasize higher education as a destination;
- they sustain conventional perceptions of further and higher education, rather than seeking to change them.

Access to and through further and higher education for adult students lacking the conventional entry qualifications is possible by many other means than access courses (Michaels 1986; National Institute of Adult Continuing Education 1989). These include access through examination or assessment, through liberal adult education provision, through the assessment of prior learning, through probationary enrolment, and through open entry schemes (see the discussions of open and experiential learning in Chapter 5, and of accreditation later in this chapter). All British institutions of further and higher education currently use one or more of these methods, sometimes in combination.

The effect of equating access narrowly with access courses, and ignoring these other, long-standing alternatives, may actually be a reduction in overall accessibility and participation (Wright 1991). Some institutions of higher education may be only too willing to accept access courses as the sole means for admitting otherwise underqualified adults. That would enable them to discontinue other, more flexible and diverse, methods of enabling wider access. It would also deny the fuller meaning of the term access.

ACCREDITATION AND MODULARIZATION

The twin concepts of modularization and accreditation are central to many contemporary discussions about adult education and training. They also encapsulate two key issues in the structuring of learning experiences by educational and other institutions:

- How should the learning experience be ordered?
- How should the learning experience be assessed?

Thus, while modularization is an increasingly common response to the first of these questions, so accreditation of the resulting modules, or their equivalents, represents at least a partial answer to the second.

At the basis of the concept of modularization is the idea that educational or training provision should be organized in terms of a series of modules:

> A *module* or course unit is a self-contained block or unit of study which has a standard size or some method of agreeing a standard value. . . . *A course* comprises the range of units of study available to students leading to a particular award. . . . *A programme of studies* is an individual student's pathway through the course.
>
> (Ram 1989, p. 3)

This is not to imply, however, that there is just one standard or agreed scheme of modularization in existence. Modular systems are commonly specific to groups of institutions, individual institutions, departments or even courses. This may present problems if students wish to transfer between courses and/or institutions, with issues of equivalence frequently arising.

Different providers have also adopted modular schemes with varying degrees of enthusiasm. At one extreme is the simple recasting of an existing course, or set of courses, in a modular format, with no other changes and hence no increased flexibility for the student. Towards the other extreme are systems which modularize the whole of an institution's provision, breaking down boundaries between subjects and courses, and enabling individual students to create their own programmes of study (Squires 1986). Such systems might allow students to add their own modules through, for example, extended project work or the accreditation of prior learning (see below and the section on experiential in Chapter 5).

There is nothing particularly new, of course, about the idea of modularization. It has been common practice for many years in American colleges and universities, was adopted by the British Open University from its inception in 1969, and had been used by the University of London before then. Nevertheless:

Modularity is fashionable. The reasons are well-rehearsed –
new clients with new needs and mixed modes of study,
customer choice, credit frameworks, blurring boundaries
between academic disciplines, new integrations between
'academic' and 'vocational' programmes, the pressure of
Assessment of Prior Experiential Learning (APEL) and
National Vocational Qualifications (NVQs) – and a claimed
cost-effectiveness. The curricular case for well-designed modular programmes is also well-rehearsed – student choice,
learner autonomy, flexibility for individual student circumstances, adaptability to new modes of learning and assessment, speed of response to external pressures and agencies,
openness to new kinds of knowledge and new connections.
As with all things, however, its potential strengths are its
possible weaknesses. Poorly designed modular programmes
are vulnerable to intellectual incoherence, to problems
with continuity and progression of learning, to loss of student
identity and to excessive bureaucracy.

(Walker 1994, pp. 24–5)

The widespread adoption of modularization by adult education
and training providers in the United Kingdom and some other
countries may be linked to external pressures to increase participation rates and flexibility while simultaneously reducing unit
costs. Modular schemes may appear, at least in principle, to offer
significant advantages both to providers and participants.

Thus, they may offer 'savings' to an institution where courses
share some of the same modules, or where available spare places
may be 'infilled' from outside. However, such savings come at
some cost in terms of increased class sizes, reduced individual
attention to students and staff stress. Similarly, while modularization may offer more choice in terms of course contents to
students, this can only be realized if the restrictions on modular
combinations caused by timetabling or previous study requirements are minimized (Watson *et al.* 1989).

The most fundamental objections to modularization, however,
stem from concerns about the organization of knowledge and
loss of expert control. Many professional educators and trainers,
understandably, believe that they have a far better understanding
of what learners need, and of what is required in a course, than
the learners themselves. While this should not preclude some

flexibility and individualization of the curriculum, it suggests that, at the very least, the overall structure of the learning experience, and the pathways through it, should remain under the direct control of the educator or trainer.

From this perspective, the more flexible or open systems of modularization may be criticized as overly reductionist and lacking in coherence. After all, where learners have a largely free choice over which combination of modules to study – a state of affairs which is often derided as the 'cafeteria' approach – where does the responsibility lie for ensuring that they are able to make some overall sense of their programme of study? With the learners themselves, perhaps with some oversight? Or does this not matter that much? If the latter is the case, is the role of the educator or trainer not then reduced simply to delivering more or less arbitrary 'chunks' of learning?

Similar reservations and criticisms have been made regarding the extension of accreditation throughout the education and training system. Accreditation has to do with the recognition of what learners have learned, and has always been a major role of educators and trainers. In essence, it may be argued that the only distinct role of educational bodies – as opposed to, for example, business or community organizations – remains their ability to grant individuals qualifications or awards which have national and international standing.

The conventional and accepted approach has long been that such accreditation relates largely or exclusively to learning that has taken place under supervised conditions within a recognized educational or training institution. The current interest in accreditation has more to do with recognizing the worth of learning wherever it has taken place, and however it was gained. Accreditation in this sense is not, though, a recent innovation. Like many developments in education and training, it has come to the UK, in the last decade or so, from the USA. The original philosophy can, however, be traced back to Britain, where organizations like the University of London were behind much pioneering work (Bell and Tight 1993).

Like other policies targeted on vocational education and training (see Chapter 4), the current impetus behind the development of accreditation in Britain has much to do with the perception of the workforce as underskilled and underqualified. The wider use of accreditation systems is seen as one practical response. It allows the recognition of much existing but uncredited learning, and, perhaps more significantly, the development of more flexible means for encouraging future learning. Thus learning may be undertaken on the job, or in one's spare time, rather than requiring costly release from work. Indeed, some have gone so far as to argue for the creation of a 'credit culture' (Higher Education Quality Council 1994).

The accreditation movement has major implications, of course, for the roles of educators, trainers and the organizations for which they work. They may then become concerned not just with the accreditation of learners who have followed their own courses, but with the accreditation of any learning in their areas of expertise, whether they have been responsible for it or not. Such accredited learning may then be accepted as part of a larger programme of study, a section of which may be undertaken within the accrediting institution itself.

Many institutions and providers have become increasingly interested in systems for the accreditation of prior learning, and there have been a number of recent publications produced which aim to guide educators or trainers through the relevant processes (e.g. Challis 1993; Simosko 1991). These processes would typically include the identification of learning, selection of relevant learning, demonstration of its validity, matching of learning outcomes, assessment of the evidence presented and, if satisfactory, its accreditation. Clearly, these processes could be enlightening, but also potentially very time-consuming, both for the individual and the institution concerned. In some cases, then, it might well be argued that it would be easier, and perhaps cheaper, to undertake a course for credit rather than have prior learning accredited.

The critique of the accreditation movement goes deeper than this: there are other practical and educational objections. Like modularization, in the UK there is no one standard and nationally recognized credit system, though the work of the National Council for Vocational Qualifications may be seen as moving in this direction. From an educational point of view, the wish to accredit as much learning as possible can be seen as both limiting and offputting. It runs counter to the values espoused in the idea of liberal education (see the section 'vocational or liberal?' in Chapter 1). Thus, it has been argued that: 'credit levels construct the learner and label and define experience' (Avis 1991,

p. 40). Is the only, or the overriding, value of learning to be seen in the number and level of credit points it earns for the learner? If so, this may influence not just how we learn but what we learn, in our desire to gain those credits as quickly, easily and cheaply as possible. For many adults, such an approach would be both meaningless and stultifying.

In an increasingly competitive and uncertain working environment, accreditation for vocational purposes may be more and more essential. Yet, one of the chief delights of learning undertaken for other purposes, or for no particular purpose at all, remains the lack of pressure to engage with assessment and accreditation in any form.

SUCCESS AND DROPOUT

Most studies of adult education and training have focused either on the characteristics of the learners or on the nature of the learning opportunities made available to them. Less attention has been given to the success or otherwise of the learning experience, and the reasons for this, despite continuing concerns about the numbers of adults who fail to complete (or drop out from) courses or programmes. The whole area of evaluation has too often been regarded as of limited interest (Edwards 1991; Harris and Bell 1990), though this is changing in the light of current concerns with 'quality' (see the section on quality in Chapter 6).

Of course, assessing the relative success or failure of adult education or training is not usually a straightforward exercise. It will normally not be adequate to make a once-and-for-all judgement at the end of a given learning experience. Success and failure are relevant concepts before and at the point of entry, during the learning experience, at its completion, and afterwards. We also have to recognize that our individual perspectives on the success or failure of a learning experience – whether as learners, teachers or providers – will vary over time, so that we may, for example, only come to appreciate its value years afterwards.

Studies of the success of actual learning experiences, as they are in progress, have focused on how learners' expectations compare with the reality of their courses or programmes. Many of these studies have looked at mature students in higher education, often comparing their experiences with those of younger students (Metcalf 1993; Roberts *et al.* 1992). They have frequently identified a dissonance between the over-expectations of learners and their actual experiences, which can lead to considerable disappointment (Weil 1986). While some dissonance is to be expected, it is obviously in the interests of those concerned to find ways of minimizing and accommodating such problems.

The relative success of a formally completed learning experience, on the other hand, is most commonly and easily assessed through measuring performance in some kind of examination or test. This remains the normal approach in both conventional and competence-based forms of education and training, whether continuous, repeated or single forms of assessment are used.

As in the case of studies of progress on course, much attention here has been devoted to how the performance of adults compares with that of younger age groups. Thus, for example, studies of the progress and performance of adult students in higher education have tended to show that adults, and those with 'non-traditional' entry qualifications, are, on average, as successful in their studies as younger students (Molloy and Carroll 1992; Smithers and Griffin 1986). Given the relative care taken in the selection process, this is, perhaps, only to be expected.

It is much more difficult, of course, to assess the benefits or disbenefits of learning experiences in broader as well as non-quantitative terms. Where courses or programmes do not involve formal testing or examination, evaluation is perhaps even more important, but all too often is carried out by means of 'happy sheets', which tend to have a self-fulfilling quality about them.

More detailed and longer term studies are needed to identify the changes in attitudes, identity, quality of life and values which education, in its fullest sense, is intended to achieve (Pascarella and Terenzini 1991). Thus, a fifty-year, quantitative study of a cohort of Swedish men concluded that:

> As the direct effects of adult education on occupational status increase over time, the total effects of the former on earnings mediated by occupational status also increase with age. . . . In general, participants in adult education regard their lives as more worthwhile, full, rich and interesting than those who do not take part.
>
> (Tuijnman 1989, p. 4)

Shorter term and cross-sectional studies which have looked at the effects of education and training on employment are more common (see, for example, Boys and Kirkland 1988; Brown and Webb 1990; Tarsh 1989; see also the section on career in Chapter 4). The recent growth of interest in adult learning routes, focusing on how adults link learning experiences together, and relate them to employment and other activities, is also relevant here (McGivney 1992, 1993).

Studies of the success of learning experiences may be related to general studies of participation. Conversely, an interest in the issues of failure and/or dropout may be related to the idea of non-participation. Examining the voluntary or forced exclusion of many from access to learning opportunities, and the reasons for this, provides an inverse view to surveys of who participates (see, for example, McGivney 1990, and the section on access and participation earlier in this chapter).

So far as adult education and training are concerned, it has to be said that a large, and probably disproportionate, proportion of the effort that has been expended on measuring and understanding success or failure has been devoted to the issue of dropout. It has long been recognized, of course, that many adults who begin a programme or course of study do not complete it, and attitudes towards this have varied from the concerned to the cavalier. These variations are somewhat reflected in the different terms used to label dropout, which also include the prosaic 'non-completion', the rather stronger 'retention' and the vigorous 'attrition'.

Naturally, such dropout causes concern among many educators and trainers. Yet it may have positive as well as negative causes and consequences. Thus, a learner may leave a course because they judge that their learning needs have been satisfied, or because they have identified another course better able to satisfy them. In such cases, it is not unreasonable to regard dropout as representing a success, from the individual's if not the provider's point of view. Learners may also, and perhaps most commonly, discontinue for reasons which have little to do with the learning experience itself, but relate to other demands on their time and resources, such as employment and family.

Educators and trainers, and the institutions which employ them, are understandably keen to be able to predict, with a reasonable degree of accuracy, whether adults starting a course will complete or dropout. After all, dropout may have financial consequences for them, as well as being disruptive for other learners and their teachers or trainers. Interestingly, while British studies of dropout have tended to draw up lists of indicators (e.g. Bourner *et al.* 1991; Woodley and Parlett 1983; Woodley *et al.* 1987), the much wider body of American work has been more explicity concerned with the development and testing of explanatory theory (e.g. Bean and Metzner 1985; Cabrera *et al.* 1992; Tinto 1987). Indeed, this may be said to be one of most theorized areas of educational study.

POLICY AND RESEARCH

The discussion in this chapter reflects and reinforces many of the general issues already noted and commented upon earlier in the book. This is apparent, for example, when we consider alternative interpretations of concepts, and the actual or potential tensions between the individual and the organizational perspective. But there are also other concerns which have been particularly highlighted by the analysis presented here, though they also have more general application. Two of these concerns seem especially worthy of comment by way of conclusion: the impact of policy and the role of research.

Policy imperatives can be seen to underlie each of the three pairs of concepts examined in this chapter. They provide the stimulus for encouraging increased access to, and participation in, education and training by adults. They are the motivation for the widespread introduction of modularization, accreditation and other more flexible methods of structuring educational provision. They articulate the concern with the success or failure of learners and the programmes they follow.

The position of research is also a theme which threads its way throughout this chapter. Educational researchers have been much concerned with the questions of why individual adults participate or not in particular kinds of learning experience. They are also very exercised about why, given their decision to participate, adults may subsequently drop out from, or fail successfully to complete, their learning programmes.

Both of these factors have a dual influence on the use of concepts. At one level – particularly in the case of national policies, but also for influential research studies – they offer a single, unifying, but perhaps doctrinaire, view of what a concept means. When the government of the day, or one of the leading researchers in the field, states that a given concept has a specific meaning, it is difficult not to be influenced. But, at another, and perhaps more important level, policy development and research studies also offer a critique and a reinterpretation of others' usage and understanding of concepts.

FURTHER READING

Brennan, J (1989) 'Access courses', pp. 51–63 in O Fulton (ed.) *Access and Institutional Change*. Milton Keynes, Open University Press.
    Accessible account of the development and ideology of the British access course movement.
Courtney, S (1992) *Why Adults Learn: towards a theory of participation in adult education*. London, Routledge.
    Thorough consideration of the different approaches and theories which have been developed, so far with only partial success, to try and explain adult participation.
Higher Education Quality Council (1994) *Choosing to Change: extending access, choice and mobility in higher education*. London, HEQC.
    National report which argues at length for the adoption of a credit culture in higher education.
McGivney, V (1990) *Education's For Other People: access to education for non-participant adults*. Leicester, National Institute of Adult Continuing Education.
    Thoughtful analysis of the reasons why many adults do not participate in education, training or learning.
Pascarella, E and Terenzini, P (1991) *How College Affects Students: findings and insights from twenty years of research*. San Francisco, Jossey-Bass.
    Massive synthesis of hundreds of, mainly American, studies of the impact of higher education upon its participants.
Tight, M (1993) 'Access, not access courses: maintaining a broad vision', pp. 62–74 in R Edwards, S Sieminski and D Zeldin (eds) *Adult Learners, Education and Training*. London, Routledge.
    Critique of those who would equate the broader concept of access with the narrower concern of access courses.

Chapter 8

Conceptual understandings

CONCEPTUAL CONCLUSIONS

The intention of this final chapter is not substantially to repeat the arguments and findings of the preceding chapters. Rather, the aim is to draw from those analyses some more general conclusions, which may usefully illuminate the use and understanding of concepts in adult education and training. Hopefully, these conclusions, in drawing upon and extending the frameworks for analysis suggested in the Introduction, will provide a broad structure which will be helpful in examining other concepts or related areas of study.

This chapter contains four relatively short sections which successively and collectively summarize a series of conclusions. The sections have been labelled conceptual relations, conceptual characteristics, conceptual analyses and conceptual futures. As with the organization of the book as a whole, however, these sections are neither discrete nor entirely robust.

The first of the sections which follows briefly looks at the relationships between the kind of concepts we have been studying and five general themes: time, space, policy, theory and ideals. The second section examines three key characteristics shared by most, if not all, of the concepts included: tensions, competition and dimensions. The third section then reviews three ways in which many of the concepts considered may be analysed: in terms of social variables, organizational levels and educational linkages. Finally, the fourth section speculates a little about the future development of concepts in adult education and training.

CONCEPTUAL RELATIONS

In this section, the relationship between concepts in adult education and training and five broad themes will be considered. These
five themes are not, of course, the only ones which could have
been chosen for examination, but they are, arguably amongst the
most general in terms of application and relevance. They include
two themes, time and space (i.e. the historical and comparative
dimensions), which were anticipated in the introductory chapter.
The three other themes chosen – policy, theory and ideals – have
arisen from the analyses presented in the chapters which
followed.

Time

All of the concepts which have been examined in this book, like
all thoughts, ideas and constructs, are located in time. They all
have a history. Even where this seems to be brief, there are the
connections with other concepts of longer standing to be considered. There are a number of obvious implications which arise
from this location in time, but it is surprising just how often
these are overlooked, and how frequently individuals seem to
believe that they are advocating 'new' concepts.

Thus, because concepts are located in time, they are subject to
change and development. There are few ideas which remain
constant for any length of time. Looking backwards into history,
we may think that we can identify 'traditions', or we may have
them presented to us by others. Even these traditions, however,
represent processes rather than constancies, and are subject to
continual reinterpretation (see the section on tensions, traditions
and dichotomies in Chapter 3).

Similarly, we can detect fashions in conceptual development
and usage. Concepts have a 'sell by date'. They may rise to
prominence, be widely talked about, analysed and applied, only
to sink into relative obscurity within comparatively few years
(see, for example, human capital in Chapter 4). Or they move
from the conceptual realm to be taken as 'fact'. Thus, the selection of concepts presented for discussion in this book would
probably be different if it had been written five or ten years ago,
or in the future, though there would probably also be many
common terms included.

These changes are not simply one way: in other words, concepts do not just rise, fall and disappear from usage. They are often reused or recycled once or more times throughout their history, sometimes wittingly, at other times unconsciously. This may or may not involve a change in the wording of the concept, or perhaps even the complete substitution of one concept for another of essentially the same meaning (see, for example, open in Chapter 5).

Space

Clearly, space complements time as the other obvious dimension in which to understand the location of concepts. Just as the application and meaning of concepts varies throughout history, and has its own history, so conceptual usage and understanding differs from place to place, and country to country. It has an international or comparative dimension.

These spatial variations in conceptual usage can be partly traced, of course, to differences in language and culture. Thus, as has been stressed a number of times in the text, the focus in this book has been primarily on anglophone concepts; those which have developed in the English, and latterly American, systems. Other linguistic and cultural traditions, such as the francophone, have produced and used rather different series of concepts, though in many cases these are analogous (see, for example, lifelong and recurrent in Chapter 2).

Yet we live in an increasingly internationalized world, and in some ways our ideas and practices are coming closer and closer together. Or, at least, our understanding of others' ideas and practices is improving. Hence, particularly with the post-war rise in the influence of a range of international organizations, many more concepts are coming to have global application and meaning. This does not appear, however, to be happening as quickly in adult education and training as in some other fields, such as the pure sciences, largely because of its relatively under-developed character and low status.

Policy

All governments, political parties and interest groups make widespread use of concepts. Indeed, it could be said that concepts are central to politics, whether these are driven by ideological concerns or more pragmatic policy-making interests. Concepts offer convenient, and superficially simple, labels for more complex ideas, which can then be sold to voters or used to rally supporters (see, for example, the discussion of capability and enterprise in Chapter 6).

This is not to say that politicians or policy-makers actually create concepts themselves; this rarely seems to be the case. What tends to happen is that they adopt and adapt concepts which are available, and which appear to connect with the ideas and policies they are working with. The meaning and application of these concepts may then be changed quite radically, as in the case of continuing education (see adult and continuing in Chapter 3). A new vocabulary for presenting and analysing them may also be developed.

Where concepts are being used politically in these ways, they will then tend to become the subject of much broader discussion and debate (see, for example, learning society in Chapter 2). They may enter popular discussion, rather than being limited to academic or political circles, and be further developed as a result.

Theory

Concepts also have a close linkage with our ways of furthering our understanding of our world. They can provide a focus for research and theory development. They are used to encapsulate our ideas about what is particularly important or significant in any one area of interest (see, for example, andragogy in Chapter 5). They offer a means to both organize and explain our concerns.

This is why it is so important for those who routinely handle concepts to have a better understanding of their meaning and application. Offering such an understanding is, of course, the fundamental purpose of this book. Without a broader and deeper view, it would be so easy to interpret concepts solely from one's own, inevitably relatively narrow, perspective.

Concepts also have an important enabling function so far as theory development and research are concerned. Labelling a set of issues or ideas as a concept (see, for example, the discussion of career in Chapter 4, or of experiential in Chapter 5) effectively legitimates, and to some extent demarcates, them as an area for investigation. This is a key way by which disciplinary knowledge develops.

Ideals

Just as concepts may be linked to ideology by way of their role in politics, so may they be connected with ideals. Ideals and ideology are closely related terms, of course, and may in practice derive from each other. Here, however, the term 'ideals' is being used in a broader and less political sense. For concepts may be presented as ideals or ideal types to be aimed for, as hopeful aspirations, or even as utopias (see the section on ideals and fashions in Chapter 2).

In this sense, some concepts represent unreal and unachievable ideas (see, for example,the discussion of the learning organization in Chapter 2, and of independent and self-directed learning in Chapter 5). Their status as ideals does not necessarily mean, however, that they are of no practical value. They may offer a model or target against which progress and practice may be judged, even if it can never be totally emulated. Concepts may be a process rather than a product. As such, they can have a valid, inspirational role.

In a similar way, some concepts may encapsulate an ideal (for example, quality, discussed in Chapter 6) which is not so much unachievable as ill-defined. In such cases, the concept's role may be to stimulate concern and direct attention. A detailed and pragmatic working out of what the concept may mean in a given context and situation may then follow, which can then allow it to be better achieved in practice.

CONCEPTUAL CHARACTERISTICS

In addition to sharing varied relations with the themes of time, space, policy, theory and ideals, as just discussed, all of the concepts in adult education and training analysed in this book have other characteristics in common. These relate to the concepts themselves rather than their contexts. Three key characteristics will be briefly considered in this section: the tendency of concepts to exhibit tensions, their competitive status, and their positioning within dimensions.

Tensions

Part of the role of concepts could be said to be about the recognition and structuring of tensions between differing ideas or perspectives. These tensions exist both within and between the concepts themselves.

An example of the latter would be the varied use of cognate ideas like distance, open and flexible education, learning or training (see Chapter 5). In this case, it is not altogether clear which is the most general concept, to what extent they duplicate each other, and how best they might be seen as related. We might, for example, view distance learning as either a precursor or a part of open learning. Open and flexible learning, on the other hand, both seem equally all-encompassing, and might be seen as synonymous.

Interestingly, each of these three concepts also presupposes the existence of a paired but opposed 'shadow' concept. The term 'shadow' concept is used since it is rarely articulated as such, or at least not to the same extent. These we might call face-to-face, closed and inflexible education, learning or training. Some other examples of shadow concepts are suggested in Figure 8.1, and many more might be derived by speculating from this book's list of contents.

For an example of tensions within a concept, the notions of development (see Chapter 1) and success (see Chapter 7) may be used. In the case of development, there is an essential internal tension between personal and economic interpretations of the

Distance education	Face-to-face education
Open learning	Closed learning
Flexible training	Inflexible training
Development	Stasis
Community	Conflict
Knowledge	Ignorance
Access	Exclusion

Figure 8.1 Concepts and shadow concepts

concept. In the case of success, there are tensions between simple completion and other possible measures, such that the concept may be interpreted in myriad and individual ways.

This review of tensions immediately illustrates a series of other common conceptual characteristics. Thus, instead of having somewhat hidden shadows, they may be set up as dichotomies. Examples include education/training and teaching/learning (see Chapter 1, and also the discussion of knowledge and skill in Chapter 6, especially Figure 6.1). In some cases, the distinctions being made may be more than twofold: for example, the three-fold trichotomy, formal/non-formal/informal (discussed in Chapter 3). Hence, while concepts perform the function of encapsulating important ideas, they are also about making divisions and distinctions (see, for example, the case of professional, discussed in Chapter 4). They have a dual role of inclusion and exclusion. From this point of view, it may be equally as useful to be able to say that something is not, for example, education, as it is to be able to confirm that it is.

Competition

The discussion of tensions within and between concepts slides naturally into a recognition, in many cases, of their competitive status. Various gradations may be recognized here. Thus, there may be competitive views taken of the same concept (see, for example, the alternative views taken of open, discussed in Chapter 5).

Competition can also be seen as occurring between concepts which occupy much the same area of discussion, as in the case of experiential and self-directed (examined in Chapter 5). Or it may be that similar concepts are deliberately advanced by organizations or interests to compete with each other. Revealing examples of this trend are the use of lifelong and recurrent education (see Chapter 2), and of capability and enterprise (reviewed in Chapter 6).

In many cases, including most of those just instanced, such competition is a partial and temporary phenomenon. After all, the advocates of competing concepts of these kinds will tend to share much the same ideas, and favour similar responses to the same issues. After a period of more overt competition, therefore, the use of such concepts is likely to become mutually reinforcing and supportive, such that their meaning and application may be almost indistinguishable to subsequent generations or audiences.

There are other instances, however, where the competition between concepts is more deep rooted and thus longer lasting. The most obvious example among those discussed in this book is that between vocational and liberal views of education and training (discussed in Chapter 1). Here, the concepts are being used to label, advance and contest alternative perspectives of the whole field.

Dimensions

In practice, of course, the position is usually rather more complicated than that. People rarely advocate only vocational education, or only liberal education. If they do, they tend to be using the terms in a more general and inclusive fashion. Courses are neither wholly open nor wholly closed. Such concepts represent positions on a continuum, spectrum or dimension (see the discussion of the relations between education, learning and training in Chapter 1, and particularly Figure 1.2).

Thus, open–closed offers one dimension – and also, as already suggested, a dichotomy – for judging educational provision or learning experiences. This is a dimension on which all practical examples would be located away from the extreme poles of wholly open and wholly closed. Similarly, any example of education, learning or training is likely to mix elements of the vocational and liberal approaches.

Once we recognize the positioning of concepts along a variety of possible dimensions, it becomes easier to appreciate how they may overlap in certain areas, slide into each other, or even substitute one for the other. Thus, while in many instances it may be relatively easy to justify why we view a given example as education or learning, or as further rather than higher education (see Chapters 1 and 3), in other cases we might not be so sure. Though concepts may be about exclusion as well as inclusion, and may be presented as competitive terms or dichotomies, their boundaries are not necessarily precise, and are subject to perception, negotiation, interpretation and change.

CONCEPTUAL ANALYSES

The discussion so far, in the preceding chapters as well as in this one, has indicated a range of different ways in which concepts in adult education and training may be considered and analysed. The purpose of this section is to look at three particular ways (or groups of ways) by which conceptual analysis might be approached. These are in terms of underlying social variables, organizational levels or educational linkages. The first two of these methods were suggested in the Introduction (see the section on frameworks for analysis); while the third was prominent in Chapter 3.

Social variables

The consideration of underlying social variables (e.g. gender, race, class, age, etc.) in the analysis of any issue is at the heart of the social science approach. It is just as valid in the analysis of the use of concepts.

In the case of gender, for example, we have seen how the interpretation of concepts like career and skill (discussed in Chapters 4 and 6), and indeed of any work-related concept, is rooted in our varying ideas of the roles and positions of men and women in society. A conventional view might equate work with full-time, continuing and paid employment, and thus take an implicitly male perspective. Other, broader views, building on the work of feminist authors, are, however, possible, useful and revealing.

The issue of age, to take a second example, underpins all discussion about adult education and training, at least implicitly. The very field of adult education and training itself is, after all, defined in distinction from child and/or youth education and training. Though adulthood constitutes the great majority of our lifespans, at least in the industrialized world, it is still quite possible to discuss adults as if they were a homogeneous group, and this is a tendency which has to be guarded against. Age, or more broadly time, is, however, explicit in many of the concepts which have been examined; including, for example, development, lifelong, recurrent, continuing, career and experiential (see Chapters 1, 2, 3, 4 and 5). These encapsulate the idea of changes during the adult's lifespan.

Organizational levels

Many of the concepts discussed in this book may be considered in terms of different organizational levels or statuses. The three-fold categorization most commonly used has been that which recognizes the levels of the individual, the organization and the society. This typology may, however, be modified and added to. We might think in terms of the group or the community, as well as the organization, as lying between the individual and society levels. The descriptors local, regional, national and international (or global) could be used as an alternative classification, usefully bringing in a recognition of the role of governments and states, as well as of the comparative element.

Some of the concepts which have been reviewed relate only or chiefly to just one of these levels. Thus the learning organization refers primarily to the organizational level, while the learning society is concerned with the societal level (see Chapter 2). Other concepts can be interpreted at two levels. For example, career may be seen from the perspective of the individual or of the organization, while human capital may be interpreted at the individual or societal level (both of these concepts are discussed in Chapter 4).

In other cases, it is possible, and indeed sensible, to analyse single concepts or series of concepts at a variety of levels. The ideas of access and participation (examined in Chapter 7), for example, may each be approached from the point of view of the individual learner, of the educational or employing organization, and of society as a whole.

Alternatively, a series of concepts may enable an analysis of a linked succession of organizational levels. This is perhaps clearest in the case of the international concepts already referred to: lifelong learning, the learning organization, the learning society (explored in Chapter 2). These can be seen as articulating shared concerned at, respectively, the individual, organizational and societal levels of analysis.

Educational linkages

As the discussion of age in the sub-section on social variables above has already indicated, it is difficult to proceed far in an analysis of concepts in adult education without referring to non-adult, that is child and youth, education and training. This is partly a question of definition, and partly a matter of linkage between these two broad areas.

There is, of course, no clear and absolute division between adult and non-adult forms of education and training. This was shown in the analysis of the terms post-compulsory, post-initial, post-secondary and post-school in Chapter 3 (see the section on the institutional framework). Adulthood cannot be defined solely in terms of age (as suggested in the section on adult education in Chapter 1), and there are too many overlaps in provision and practice between adult and non-adult education and training. So there are inevitably some shared concerns which extend across the porous and indefinite boundaries we manage to recognize.

The linkages are, however, much stronger and more complex than that. Non-adult and adult forms of education and training are arranged in a sequential fashion, even if there are gaps, so that almost all of those involved as participants as adults will have also participated as children and youths.

The nature of adult education and training is, therefore, largely a reaction or response to what is provided for children. It may take the form of supplementary education, intended to overcome deficiencies in child or youth learning. Or it may be progressional, building upon and extending what has already been learned (see the section on further and higher education in Chapter 3). Whichever the case, those involved in delivering or understanding adult education and training cannot afford to ignore developments in child and youth provision.

CONCEPTUAL FUTURES

What might, then, be said about the possible future development of concepts in adult education and training? Clearly, anything suggested here must be more or less speculative, but that need not hold us back too much.

The first point to make here, however, is that the context for adult education and training as a field of study is unlikely to change much in the foreseeable future. Adult education and training does not have disciplinary status, and, as suggested in the Introduction (see the section on frameworks for analysis), derives many of its ideas from a range of other established academic disciplines, such as economics, psychology and sociology.

The concepts used, and their interpretations, reflect this status and these linkages. So it may be advisable to try and predict what is likely to happen in these related disciplines before speculating about future conceptual developments in adult education and training.

That aside, I (and here the first person intervenes for the first time since the Introduction) would expect many of the following conceptual developments to take place in the future:

- a continuing recycling, reinterpretation and renaming of many existing concepts;
- a continuation of the vocational/liberal tension in conceptual discussions, with the emphasis moving back some way towards the liberal perspective at some point in the not too distant future;
- a good deal of conceptual activity, stimulated by the growing policy debate, around the ideas of the learning organization and the learning society;
- the development and popularization of additional concepts to do with further, higher, adult and continuing education and training, reflecting both the expansion and diversification of these areas of provision;
- a growth in the area of work-related concepts, building upon the increasing prevalence of linkages between education and work;
- the effective rejection of the idea of andragogy, and its replacement by other proto-theories to explain and understand adult education and training;
- considerable activity around the concepts of competence and quality, better to define and critically assess their meanings and application;
- further work on the ideas of success and failure, and outcomes, more adequately to recognize the multiple routes which are possible through and beyond education and training.

TOWARDS LEARNERSHIP

From my own perspective, I would like to do more, and see more done, on two related areas of analysis:

1   the links between education and training and aspects of life
     other than work;
2   the sequential and cumulative educational and training
     experiences which individual adults have throughout their
     lives.

If, therefore, I were to offer a single concept for development,
popularization and analysis, it would be something like 'learnership'. My apologies if someone has already thought of this –
they probably have – and I have contrived to overlook their
work.

The concept of learnership would refer to two aspects of adult
education and training. First, it would recognize the active and
continuing engagement of certain adults in learning, both over
a considerable period of time and in a range of different settings.
Second, it would reinforce these adults' recognition of this
activity as an important, valid, related and integral engagement
alongside other major life roles like worker, parent and partner.

Such a concept would, hopefully, help to raise the status of
the whole field of adult education and training.

References

Advisory Council for Adult and Continuing Education (1982) *Continuing Education: From Policies to Practice.* Leicester, ACACE.

Ainley, P (1994) *Degrees of Difference: Higher Education in the 1990s.* London, Lawrence and Wishart.

Allen, I (1994) *Doctors and Their Careers: A New Generation.* London, Policy Studies Institute.

Allman, P (1983) 'The nature and process of adult development', pp. 107–23 in M Tight (ed.) *Adult Learning and Education.* London, Croom Helm.

Argyris, C (1982) *Reasoning, Learning and Action: Individual and Organizational.* San Francisco, Jossey-Bass.

—— *On Organizational Learning.* Oxford, Blackwell.

Argyris, C and Schön, D (1976) *Theory in Practice: Increasing Professional Effectiveness.* San Francisco, Jossey-Bass.

—— (1978) *Organizational Learning: A Theory of Action Perspective.* Reading, Massachusetts, Addison-Wesley.

Arthur, M, Hall, D and Lawrence, B (1989) 'Generating new directions in career theory: the case for a transdisciplinary approach', pp. 7–25 in M Arthur, D Hall and B Lawrence (eds) *Handbook of Career Theory.* Cambridge, University Press.

Ashworth, A and Harvey, R (1994) *Assessing Quality in Further and Higher Education.* London, Jessica Kingsley.

Ashworth, P and Saxton, J (1990) 'On competence'. *Journal of Further and Higher Education,* 14, 2, pp. 3–25.

Avis, J (1991) 'Not so radical after all? Access, credit levels and the learner'. *Journal of Access Studies,* 6, 1, pp. 40–51.

Bååth, J (1981) 'On the nature of distance education'. *Distance Education,* 2, 2, pp. 212–19.

Bagley, B and Challis, B (1985) *Inside Open Learning.* Coombe Lodge, Further Education Staff College.

Bagnall, R (1990) 'Lifelong education: the institutionalization of an illiberal and regressive concept?' *Educational Philosophy and Theory,* 22, 1, pp. 1–7.

Bailey, C (1992) 'Enterprise and liberal education: some reservations'.

Journal of the Philosophy of Education, 26, 1, pp. 99–106.

Ball, C (1990) *More Means Different: Widening Access to Higher Education*. London, Royal Society of Arts.

Ball, S, and Goodson, I (eds) (1985) *Teachers' Lives and Careers*. London, Falmer Press.

Banks, M, Bates, I, Breakwell, G, Bynner, J, Euler, N, Jamieson, L and Roberts, K (1992) *Careers and Identities*. Buckingham, Open University Press.

Barnett, R (1990) *The Idea of Higher Education*. Buckingham, Open University Press.

— (1994) *The Limits of Competence: Knowledge, Higher Education and Society*. Buckingham, Open University Press.

Barnett, R, Parry, G, Cox, R, Loder, C and Williams, G (1994) *Assessment of the Quality of Higher Education: A Review and an Evaluation*. London, Institute of Education.

Barrow, R and Milburn, G (1990) *A Critical Dictionary of Educational Concepts: An Appraisal of Selected Ideas and Issues in Educational Theory and Practice*. Hemel Hempstead, Harvester Wheatsheaf, second edition.

Barrow, R and White, P (eds) (1993) *Beyond Liberal Education: Essays in Honour of Paul Hirst*. London, Routledge.

Bartholomew, D (ed.) (1976) *Manpower Planning*. Harmondsworth, Penguin.

Bean, J and Metzner, B (1985) 'A conceptual model of nontraditional undergraduate student attrition'. *Review of Educational Research*, 55, 4, pp. 485–540.

Becher, T (1994) 'The state and the university curriculum in Britain'. *European Journal of Education*, 29, 3, pp. 231–45.

Becker, G (1993) *Human Capital: A Theoretical and Empirical Analysis with Special Reference to Education*. Chicago, University of Chicago Press. third edition.

Bees, M and Swords, M (eds) (1990) *National Vocational Qualifications and Further Education*. London, Kogan Page.

Bélanger, P (1991) 'Adult education in the industrialised countries'. *Prospects*, 21, 4, pp. 491–500.

Bell, D (1973) *The Coming of Post-industrial Society: A Venture in Social Forecasting*. New York, Basic Books.

Bell, R and Tight, M (1993) *Open Universities: A British Tradition?* Buckingham, Open University Press.

Bengtsson, J (1989) 'Recurrent education', pp. 43–51 in C Titmus (ed.) *Lifelong Education for Adults: An International Handbook*. Oxford, Pergamon.

Benner, P (1984) *From Novice to Expert: Excellence and Power in Clinical Nursing*. Menlo Park, California, Addison–Wesley.

Bennett, R and McCoshan, A (1993) *Enterprise and Human Resource Development: Local Capacity Building*. London, Paul Chapman.

Bines, H and Watson, D (1992) *Developing Professional Education*. Buckingham, Open University Press.

Birch, D and Latcham, J (1984) *Managing Open Learning*. Coombe Lodge,

Further Education Staff College.

Blackledge, D and Hunt, B (1985) *Sociological Interpretations of Education*. London, Routledge.

Blaug, M (1992) *The Methodology of Economics: Or How Economists Explain*. Cambridge, Cambridge University Press, second edition.

Blaxter, L and Tight, M (1994) 'Juggling with time: how adults manage their time for lifelong learning'. *Studies in the Education of Adults*, 26, 2, pp. 162–79.

Bligh, D (1990) *Higher Education*. London, Cassell.

Bloom, B (ed.) (1956) *Taxonomy of Educational Objectives: The Classification of Educational Goals*. New York, Longman, two volumes.

Boot, R and Hodgson, V (1987) 'Open learning: meaning and experience', pp. 5–15 in V Hodgson, S Mann and R Snell (eds) *Beyond Distance Teaching Towards Open Learning*. Milton Keynes, Open University Press.

Boshier, R *et al.* (1980) *Towards a Learning Society: New Zealand Adult Education in Transition*. Auckland, Learning Press.

Bosworth, D (1991) *Open Learning*. London, Cassell.

Boud, D, Cohen, R and Walker, D (eds) (1993) *Using Experience for Learning*. Buckingham, Open University Press.

Boud, D and Higgs, J (1993) 'Bringing self-directed learning into the mainstream of tertiary education'. pp. 158–73 in N Graves (ed.) *Learner Managed Learning: Practice, Theory and Policy*. Leeds, Higher Education for Capability.

Boud, D, Keogh, R and Walker, D (1985) 'Promoting reflection in learning: a model', pp. 18–40 in D Boud, R Keogh and D Walker (eds) *Reflection: Turning Experience into Learning*. London, Kogan Page.

Bourdieu, P and Passeron, J-C (1990) *Reproduction in Education, Society and Culture*. London, Sage, second edition, translated by R Nice.

Bourner, T, Reynolds, A, Hamed, M and Barnett, R (1991) *Part-time Students and Their Experience of Higher Education*. Buckingham, Open University Press.

Bowles, S and Gintis, H (1976) *Schooling in Capitalist America: Educational Reform and the Contradictions of Economic Life*. London, Routledge.

Boydell, T (1976) *Experiential Learning*. Manchester, University of Manchester Department of Adult Education.

Boys, C and Kirkland, J (1988) *Degrees of Success: Career Aspirations and Destinations of College, University and Polytechnic Graduates*. London, Jessica Kingsley.

Bradshaw, D (1992) 'Classifications and models of transferable skills'. pp. 39–115 in H Eggins (ed.) *Arts Graduates, Their Skills and Their Employment*. London, Falmer Press.

Brady, L (1985) *Models and Methods of Teaching*. Sydney, Prentice-Hall.

Brannen, J and Moss, P (1991) *Managing Mothers: Dual Earner Households after Maternity Leave*. London, Unwin Hyman.

Brennan, J (1989) 'Access courses', pp. 51–63 in O Fulton (ed.) *Access and Institutional Change*. Milton Keynes, Open University Press.

Bridges, D (1993) 'Transferable skills: a philosophical perspective'. *Studies in Higher Education*, 18, 1, pp. 43–51.

Brookfield, S (1981) 'Independent adult learning'. *Studies in Adult Education*, 13, pp. 15–27.

—— (1982) *Independent Adult Learning*. Nottingham, University of Nottingham Department of Adult Education.

—— (1983) *Adult Learners, Adult Education and the Community*. Milton Keynes, Open University Press.

—— (1984) 'Self-directed adult learning: a critical paradigm'. *Adult Education Quarterly*, 35, 2, pp. 59–71.

—— (1986) *Understanding and Facilitating Adult Learning*. San Francisco, Jossey-Bass.

Brown, A and Webb, J (1990) 'The higher education route to the labour market for mature students'. *British Journal of Education and Work*, 4, 1, pp. 5–21.

Brown, D (1984) 'Summary, comparison and critique of major theories', pp. 311–36 in D Brown *et al.*, *Career Choice and Development: Applying Contemporary Theories to Practice*. San Francisco, Jossey-Bass.

Buckley, R and Caple, J (1990) *The Theory and Practice of Training*. London, Kogan Page.

Burgess, T (ed.) (1986) *Education for Capability*. Windsor, NFER-Nelson.

Burgoyne, J, Pedler, M and Boydell, T (eds) (1994) *Towards the Learning Company: Concepts and Practices*. Maidenhead, McGraw-Hill.

—— (ed.) (1989) *Competency Based Education and Training*. London, Falmer Press.

—— (1991) 'Competence and higher education: implications for institutions and professional bodies', pp. 22–46 in P Raggatt and L Unwin (eds) *Change and Intervention: Vocational Education and Training*. London, Falmer Press.

—— (1995) *Outcomes, Learning and the Curriculum: Implications for NVQs, GNVQs and Other Qualifications*. London, Falmer Press.

Burnard, P (1988) 'Experiential learning: some theoretical considerations'. *International Journal of Lifelong Education*, 7, 2, pp. 127–33.

Burton, L (ed.) (1992) *Developing Resourceful Humans: Adult Education within the Economic Context*. London, Routledge.

Bynner, J (1992) 'The rise of open learning: a UK approach to work-related education and training'. *International Journal of Lifelong Education*, 11, 2, pp. 103–14.

Cabrera, A, Castañeda, M, Nara, A and Hengstler, D (1992) 'The convergence between two theories of college persistence'. *Journal of Higher Education*, 63, 2, pp. 143–64.

Campanelli, P, Channell, J, McAulay, L, Renouf, A and Thomas, R (1994) *Training: An Exploration of the Word and the Concept with an Analysis of the Implications for Survey Design*. Sheffield, Employment Department.

Candy, P, Harri-Augstein, S and Thomas, L (1985) 'Reflection and the self-organised learner: a model of learning conversations', pp. 100–16 in D Boud, R Keogh and D Walker (ed.) *Reflection: Turning Experience into Learning*. London, Kogan Page.

Cantor, L and Roberts, I (1986) *Further Education Today: A Critical Review*. London, Routledge and Kegan Paul, third edition.

Carnegie Commission on Higher Education (1973) *Towards a Learning Society: Alternative Channels to Life, Work and Service.* New York, McGraw-Hill.

Carnevale, A (1992) 'Human capital: a high-yield investment', pp. 48–71 in L Burton (ed.) *Developing Resourceful Humans: Adult Education within the Economic Context.* London, Routledge.

Centre for Educational Research and Innovation (1973) *Recurrent Education: A Strategy for Lifelong Learning.* Paris, Organization for Economic Cooperation and Development.

—— (1975) *Recurrent Education: Trends and Issues.* Paris, Organization for Economic Cooperation and Development.

Chadwick, G (1993) 'Towards a vision of recurrent education'. *Journal of Access Studies,* 8, 1, pp. 8–26.

Challis, M (1993) *Introducing APEL.* London, Routledge.

Chapman, P (1993) *The Economics of Training.* London, Harvester Wheatsheaf.

Clark, D (1987) 'The concept of community education', pp. 50–69 in G Allen, J Bastiani, I Martin and K Richards (eds) *Community Education: An Agenda for Educational Reform.* Milton Keynes, Open University Press.

Coffield, F (1990) 'From the decade of enterprise culture to the decade of TECs'. *British Journal of Education and Work,* 4, 1, pp. 59–78.

Commission on Post-secondary Education in Ontario (1972) *The Learning Society.* Toronto, Ministry of Government Services.

Committee of Inquiry (Russell Report) (1973) *Adult Education: A Plan for Development.* London, HMSO.

Committee on Higher Education (Robbins Report) (1963) *Report.* London, HMSO, Cmnd 2154.

Connelly, B (1991) 'Access or access? A framework for interpretation'. *Journal of Access Studies,* 6, 2, pp. 135–46.

Cookson, P (1986) 'A framework for theory and research on adult education participation'. *Adult Education Quarterly,* 36, 3, pp. 130–41.

Coombs, P (1968) *The World Educational Crisis: A Systems Analysis.* Oxford, Oxford University Press.

—— (1985) *The World Crisis in Education: The View from the Eighties.* Oxford, Oxford University Press.

Coombs, P and Ahmed, M (1974) *Attacking Rural Poverty: How Nonformal Education Can Help.* Baltimore, Johns Hopkins University Press.

Council for National Academic Awards (1989) *Access Courses to Higher Education: A Framework of National Arrangements for Recognition.* London, CNAA.

Council of Europe (1973) *Permanent Education: The Basis and Essentials.* Paris, Council of Europe.

—— (1975) *Permanent Education: A Framework for Recurrent Education.* Paris, Council of Europe.

Courtney, S (1992) *Why Adults Learn: Towards a Theory of Participation in Adult Education.* London, Routledge.

Craft, A (ed.) (1994) *Quality Assurance in Higher Education: Proceedings of an International Conference.* London, Falmer Press.

Critten, P (1993) *Investing in People: Towards Corporate Capability*. London, Butterworth-Heinemann.

Crombie, A and Harries-Jenkins, G (1983) *The Demise of the Liberal Tradition: Two Essays on the Future of British University Adult Education*. Leeds, University of Leeds, Department of Adult and Continuing Education.

Cropley, A (1979) 'Introduction', pp. 1–7 in A Cropley (ed.) *Lifelong Education: A Stocktaking*. Hamburg, UNESCO Institute for Education,
—— (1980) 'Lifelong learning and systems of education: an overview', pp. 1–15 in A Cropley (ed.) *Towards a System of Lifelong Education: Some Practical Considerations*. Oxford, Pergamon Press.

Cross, K (1981) *Adults as Learners: Increasing Participation and Facilitating Learning*. San Francisco, Jossey-Bass.

Cummings, W (1995) 'The Asian human resource approach in global perspective'. *Oxford Review of Education*, 21, 1, pp. 67–81.

Curzon, L (1990) *Teaching in Further Education: An Outline of Principles and Practice*. London, Cassell, fourth edition.

Cytrynbaum, S and Crites, J (1989) 'The utility of adult developmental theory in understanding career adjustment process', pp. 66–88 in M Arthur, D Hall and B Lawrence (eds) *Handbook of Career Theory*. Cambridge, Cambridge University Press.

Dale, M (1993) *Developing Management Skills*. London, Kogan Page.

Darkenwald, G and Merriam, S (1982) *Adult Education: Foundations of Practice*. New York, Harper and Row.

Dave, R (ed.) (1976) *Foundations of Lifelong Education*. Oxford, Pergamon Press.

Davenport, J (1987) 'Is there any way out of the andragogy morass?'. *Lifelong Learning: An Omnibus of Practice and Research*, 2, 3, pp. 17–20.

Davies, P (ed.) (1995) *Adults in Higher Education: International Experiences in Access and Participation*. London, Jessica Kingsley.

Dearden, R (1984) 'Education and Training'. *Westminster Studies in Education*, 7, pp. 57–66.

Debling, G and Hallmark, A (1990) 'Identification and assessment of underpinning knowledge and understanding in the context of the UK government's standards programme', pp. 8–11 in H Black and A Wolf (eds) *Knowledge and Competence: Current Issues in Training and Education*. Sheffield, Employment Department.

Department of Education and Science (1980) *Continuing Education: Post-experience Vocational Provision for Those in Employment*. London, DES.

Department of Employment (1991) *Flexible Learning: A Framework for Education and Training in the Skills Decade*. Sheffield, DE.

Dex, S (1987) *Women's Occupational Mobility: A Lifetime Perspective*. London, Macmillan.
—— (ed.) (1991) *Life and Work History Analyses: Qualitative and Quantitative Developments*. London, Routledge.

Dixon, N (1994) *The Organizational Learning Cycle: How We Can Learn Collectively*. Maidenhead, McGraw-Hill.

Doherty, G (ed.) (1994a) *Developing Quality Systems in Education*. London, Routledge.

— (1994b) 'The concern for quality', pp. 3–34 in G Doherty (ed.) *Developing Quality Systems in Education*. London, Routledge.

Dore, R (1976) *The Diploma Disease*. London, Allen and Unwin.

Dreyfus, H, Dreyfus, S and Athanasiou, T (1986) *Mind Over Machine: The Power of Human Intuition and Expertise in the Era of the Computer*. Oxford, Blackwell.

Ecclestone, K (1994) 'Democratic values and purposes: the overlooked challenge of competence'. *Educational Studies*, 20, 2, pp. 155–66.

Economic and Social Research Council (1994) *Research Specification for the ESRC 'Learning Society: knowledge and skills for employment' Programme*. Swindon, ESRC.

Edwards, J (1991) *Evaluation in Adult and Further Education: A Practical Handbook for Teachers and Organisers*. Liverpool, Workers' Educational Association.

Edwards, R (1993) *Mature Women Students: Separating or Connecting Family and Education*. London, Taylor and Francis.

Edwards, R (1995) 'Behind the Banner: whither the learning society?'. *Adults Learning, 6*, 6, pp. 187–9.

Ellis, R (ed.) (1993) *Quality Assurance in University Teaching*. Buckingham, Open University Press.

Entwistle, N and Ramsden, P (1983) *Understanding Student Learning*. London, Croom Helm.

Eraut, M (1990) 'Identifying the knowledge which underpins performance', pp. 22–8 in H Black and A Wolf (eds) *Knowledge and Competence: Current Issues in Training and Education*. Sheffield, Employment Department.

— (1994) *Developing Professional Knowledge and Competence*. London, Falmer Press.

Erdos, R (1967) *Teaching by Correspondence*. London, Longman/ UNESCO.

Eurich, N (1990) *The Learning Industry: Education for Adult Workers*. Princeton, New Jersey, Carnegie Foundation for the Advancement of Teaching.

Evans, B (1987) *Radical Adult Education: A Political Critique*. London, Croom Helm.

Evans, N (1992) *Experiential Learning: Assessment and Accreditation*. London, Routledge.

— (1994) *Experiential Learning for All*. London, Routledge.

Evans, T and Nation, D (1992) 'Theorising open and distance learning'. *Open Learning*, 7, 2, pp. 3–13.

Evetts, J (ed.) (1994) *Women and Career: Themes and Issues in Advanced Industrialised Societies*. Harlow, Longman.

Fairbairn, A (1971) *The Leicestershire Community Colleges*. Leicester, National Institute of Adult Education.

Fauré, E, Herrera, F, Kaddowa, A, Lopes, H, Petrovsky, A, Rahnema, M and Ward, F (1972) *Learning To Be: The World of Education Today and Tomorrow*. Paris, UNESCO/Harrap.

Field, M (1993) *APL: Developing More Flexible Colleges*. London, Routledge.

Finegold, D, Keep, E, Miliband, D, Raffe, D, Spons, K and Young, M (1990) *A British 'Baccalaureat': Ending the Division between Education and Training*. London, Institute for Public Policy Research.

Fletcher, C (1980) 'The theory of community education and its relation to adult education', pp. 65–82 in J Thompson (ed.) *Adult Education for a Change*. London, Hutchinson.

— (1989) 'Community education and community development', pp. 51–4 in C Titmus (ed.) *Lifelong Education for Adults: An International Handbook*. Oxford, Pergamon.

Fletcher, S (1991) *NVQs, Standards and Competence: A Practical Guide for Employers, Managers and Trainers*. London, Kogan Page.

Flew, A (ed.) (1956) *Essays in Conceptual Analysis*. London, Macmillan.

Fordham, P (ed.) (1980) *Participation, Learning and Change: Commonwealth Approaches to Non-formal Education*. London, Commonwealth Secretariat.

— (1992) *Education For All: An Expanded Vision*. Paris, UNESCO.

Fordham, P, Poulton, G and Randle, L (1979) *Learning Networks in Adult Education: Non-Formal Education on a Housing Estate*. London, Routledge and Kegan Paul.

Foreman-Peck, L (1993) 'Enterprise education: a new social ethic for higher education'. *Vocational Aspect of Education*, 45, 2, pp. 99–111.

Forrester, K, Payne, J and Ward, K (eds.) (1993) *Developing a Learning Workforce: Conference Proceedings*. Leeds, University of Leeds, Department of Adult Continuing Education.

Foster, P (1987) 'The contribution of education to development', pp. 93–100 in G Psacharopoulos (ed.) *Economics of Education: Research and Studies*. Oxford, Pergamon.

Francis, B and Penn, R (1994) 'Towards a phenomenology of skill', pp. 223–43 in R Penn, M Rose and J Rubery (eds) *Skill and Occupational Change*. Oxford, Oxford University Press.

Freedman, L (1987) *Quality in Continuing Education: Principles, Practices and Standards for Colleges and Universities*. San Francisco, Jossey–Bass.

Freeman, R (1982) 'Flexistudy', pp. 162–5 in J Daniel, M Stroud and J Thompson (eds) *Learning at a Distance: A World Perspective*. Athabasca, Athabasca University.

— (1993) *Quality Assurance in Training and Education: How to Apply BS 5750 (ISO 9000) Standards*. London, Routledge.

Freire, P (1972) *Pedagogy of the Oppressed*. Harmondsworth, Penguin, translated by M Ramer.

— (1974) *Education for Critical Consciousness*. London, Sheed and Ward.

Fulton, O (ed.) (1989) *Access and Institutional Change*. Milton Keynes, Open University Press.

Further Education Unit (1983) *Flexible Learning Opportunities*. London, Further Education Unit.

— (1984) *Flexible Learning in Action*. London, Further Education Unit.

Gagné, R (1985) *The Conditions of Learning and Theory of Instruction*. New York, Holt, Rinehart and Winston, fourth edition.

Gallie, D and White, M (1993) *Employee Commitment and the Skills Revolution*. London, Policy Studies Institute.

Garrison, D (1989) *Understanding Distance Education: A Framework for the Future*. London, Routledge.

Garrison, D and Shale, D (1990) 'Tilting at windmills? Destroying mythology in distance education'. *International Council for Distance Education Bulletin*, 24, pp. 42–6.

Garry, A and Cowan, J (1986) *Continuing Professional Development: A Learner-centred Strategy*. London, Further Education Unit.

Gelpi, E (1979) *A Future for Lifelong Education*. Manchester, University of Manchester, Department of Adult and Higher Education, two volumes.

Gerson, K (1985) *Hard Choices: How Women Decide about Work, Career, and Motherhood*. Berkeley, University of California Press.

Gilham, B (1995) 'Moving into the open', pp. 52–61 in D Thomas (ed.) *Flexible Learning Strategies in Higher and Further Education*. London, Cassell.

Glaser, R and Chi, M (1988) 'Overview', pp. xv–xxviii in M Chi, R Glaser and M Farr (eds) *The Nature of Expertise*. Hillsdale, New Jersey, Laurence Erlbaum Associates.

Glatter, R, Wedell, E, Harris, W and Subramanian, S (1971) *Study by Correspondence: An Enquiry into Correspondence Study for Examinations for Degrees and Other Advanced Qualifications*. London, Longman.

Goldschmidt, W (1990) *The Human Career: The Self in the Symbolic World*. Oxford, Blackwell.

Goldstein, I and Gessner, M (1988) 'Training and development in work organisations'. *International Review of Industrial and Organisational Psychology*, pp. 43–72.

Graves, N (ed.) (1993) *Learner Managed Learning: Practice, Theory and Policy*. Leeds, Higher Education for Capability.

Green, D (1994) 'What is quality in higher education? Concepts, policy and practice', pp. 3–20 in D Green (ed.) *What is Quality in Higher Education*? Buckingham, Open University Press.

Griffin, C (1983) *Curriculum Theory in Adult and Lifelong Education*. London, Croom Helm.

Griffin, V (1989) 'Self-directed learning: theories', pp. 254–6 in C Titmus (ed.) *Lifelong Education for Adults: An International Handbook*. Oxford, Pergamon.

Groombridge, B (1983) 'Adult education and the education of adults', pp. 3–19 in M Tight (ed.) *Adult Learning and Education*. London, Croom Helm.

Grundy, T (1994) *Strategic Learning in Action: How to Accelerate and Sustain Business Change*. Maidenhead, McGraw-Hill.

Haggis, S (1991) *Education For All: Purpose and Context*. Paris, UNESCO.

Hakim, C (1991) 'Grateful slaves and self-made women: fact and fantasy in women's work orientations'. *European Sociological Review*, 7, 2, pp. 101–21.

Hall, D (1988) 'An overview of current career development theory, research and practice', pp. 1–20 in D Hall *et al.*, *Career Development in Organisations*. San Francisco, Jossey-Bass.

Halsey, A (1992) 'An international comparison of access to higher education'. *Oxford Studies in Comparative Education*, 1, 1, pp. 11–36.

—— (1993) 'Trends in access and equity in higher education: Britain in international perspective'. *Oxford Review of Education*, 19, 2, pp. 129–40.

Halsey, A, Heath, A and Ridge, J (1980) *Origins and Destinations: Family, Class and Education in Modern Britain*. Oxford, Clarendon Press.

Hamilton, E (1992) *Adult Education for Community Development*. Westport, Connecticut, Greenwood Press.

Harris, D (1987) *Openness and Closure in Distance Education*. London, Falmer Press.

Harris, D and Bell, C (1990) *Evaluating and Assessing for Learning*. London, Kogan Page, second edition.

Harrison, R (1988) *Training and Development*. London, Institute of Personnel Management.

—— (1992) *Employee Development*. London, Institute of Personnel Management.

Hayes, C, Fonda, N and Hillman, J (1995) *Learning in the New Millennium*. London, National Commission on Education.

Henderson, E and Nathenson, M (eds.) (1984) *Independent Learning in Higher Education*. Englewood Cliffs, Educational Technology Publications.

Her Majesty's Inspectors (1992) *A Survey of the Enterprise in Higher Education Initiative in Fifteen Polytechnics and Colleges of Higher Education, September 1989–March 1991*. London, Department of Education and Science.

Heron, J (1989) *The Facilitators' Handbook*. London, Kogan Page.

Hettne, B (1990) *Development Theory and the Three Worlds*. Harlow, Longman.

Hewitt, P (1993) *About Time: The Revolution in Work and Family Life*. London, Institute for Public Policy Research.

Hicks, N (1987) 'Education and economic growth', pp. 101–7 in G Psacharopoulos (ed.) *Economics of Education: Research and Studies*. Oxford, Pergamon.

Higher Education Quality Council (1994) *Choosing to Change: Extending Access, Choice and Mobility in Higher Education*. London, HEQC.

Hill, V (1994) *Further Education in the United Kingdom*. London, Collins Educational/Further Education Staff College, second edition.

Hirschham, L, Gilmore, T and Newell, T (1989) 'Training and learning in a post-industrial world', pp. 185–200 in H Leymann and H Kornbluh (eds) *Socialization and Learning at Work: A New Approach to the Learning Process in the Workplace and Society*. Aldershot, Avebury.

Hirst, P (1974) *Knowledge and the Curriculum: A Collection of Philosophical Papers*. London, Routledge and Kegan Paul.

Hirst, P and Peters, R (1970) *The Logic of Education*. London, Routledge.

Hobart, M (ed.) (1993) *An Anthropological Critique of Development: The Growth of Ignorance*. London, Routledge.

Hobsbawm, E and Ranger, T (eds) (1983) *The Invention of Tradition*. Cambridge, Cambridge University Press.

Hodkinson, P and Issitt, M (eds) (1995) *The Challenge of Competence: Professionalism through Vocational Education and Training*. London, Cassell.

Holloway, D (1994) 'Total quality management, the learning organisation and post-compulsory education'. *Vocational Aspect of Education*, 46, 2, pp. 117–30.

Holmberg, B (1986) *Growth and Structure of Distance Education*. Beckenham, Croom Helm.

Honey, P and Mumford, A (1986) *Manual of Learning Styles*. Reading, Peter Honey, second edition.

Houghton, V (1974) 'Recurrent education', pp. 1–9 in V Houghton, and K Richardson (eds) *Recurrent Education: A Plea for Lifelong Learning*. London, Ward Lock Educational.

Houle, C (1974) *The External Degree*. San Francisco, Jossey-Bass.

Hoyle, E and John, P (1995) *Professional Knowledge and Professional Practice*. London, Cassell.

Hughes, C and Tight, M (1995) 'The myth of the learning society'. *British Journal of Educational Studies*, 43, 3, pp. 290–304.

Husen, T (1974) *The Learning Society*. London, Methuen.

—— (1986) *The Learning Society Revisited*. Oxford, Pergamon.

Hyland, T (1994) *Competence, Education and NVQs: Dissenting Perspectives*. London, Cassell.

Illich, I (1973) *Deschooling Society*. Harmondsworth, Penguin.

Income Data Services (1994) *Employee Development Initiatives*. London, Income Data Services Ltd.

Jarvis, P (1983) *Professional Education*. London, Croom Helm.

—— (1987) *Adult Learning in the Social Context*. London, Croom Helm.

—— (1990) *An International Dictionary of Adult and Continuing Education*. London, Routledge.

—— (1995) *Adult and Continuing Education: Theory and Practice*. London, Routledge, second edition.

Jenson, D, Gray, J and Sime, N (1991) *Participation, Progress and Performance in Post-compulsory Education*. Sheffield, Employment Department.

Jessup, G (1989) 'The emerging model of vocational education and training', pp. 65–76 in J Burke (ed.) *Competency Based Education and Training*. London, Falmer Press.

—— (1991) *Outcomes: NVQs and the Emerging Model of Education and Training*. London, Falmer Press.

Johnes, G (1993) *The Economics of Education*. London, Macmillan.

Jones, A and Hendry, C (1992) *The Learning Organization: A Review of Literature and Practice*. London, HRD Partnership.

—— (1994) 'The learning organisation: adult learning and organisational transformation'. *British Journal of Management*, 5, pp. 153–62.

Jones, L and Moore, R (1993) 'Education, competence and the control of expertise'. *British Journal of the Sociology of Education*, 14, 4, pp. 385–97.

Jones, S and Joss, R (1995) 'Models of professionalism', pp. 15–33 in M Yelloly and M Henkel (eds) *Learning and Teaching in Social Work:*

Towards Reflective Practice. London, Jessica Kingsley.

Jourdan, M (ed.) (1981) *Recurrent Education in Western Europe: Progress, Projects and Trends in Recurrent, Lifelong and Continuing Education.* Slough, NFER/Nelson.

Joyce, B, Weil, M and Showers, B (1992) *Models of Teaching.* Boston, Allyn and Bacon, fourth edition.

Kallen, D (1979) 'Recurrent education and lifelong learning: definitions and distinctions', pp. 45–54 in T Schuller and J Megarry (eds) *Recurrent Education and Lifelong Learning.* London, Kogan Page.

Kanchier, C and Unruh, W (1988) 'The career cycle meets the life cycle'. *Career Development Quarterly,* 37, pp. 127–37.

Kanter, R (1989) *When Giants Learn to Dance: Mastering the Challenges of Strategy, Management and Career in the 1990s.* New York, Simon and Schuster.

Kaye, A (1988) 'Distance education: the state of the art'. *Prospects,* 18, 1, pp. 43–54.

Kaye, A and Rumble, G (eds.) (1981) *Distance Teaching for Higher and Adult Education.* Beckenham, Croom Helm.

—— (1991) 'Open universities: a comparative approach'. *Prospects,* 21, 2, pp. 214–26.

Keegan, D (1986) *The Foundations of Distance Education.* Beckenham, Croom Helm.

—— (1989) 'Problems in defining the field of distance education', pp. 8–15 in M Moore and G Clark (eds) *Readings in Principles of Distance Education.* American Center for the Study of Distance Education, Pennsylvania State University.

Kelly, A (1989) *The Curriculum: Theory and Practice.* London, Paul Chapman, third edition.

Kelly, R (1991) *The Gendered Economy: Work, Careers and Success.* London, Sage.

Kerckhoff, A (1993) *Diverging Pathways: Social Structure and Career Deflections.* Cambridge, Cambridge University Press.

Kidd, J and Titmus, C (1989) 'Introduction', pp. xxiii–xxxix in C Titmus (ed.) *Lifelong Education for Adults: An International Handbook.* Oxford, Pergamon.

Kim, D (1993) 'The link between individual and organizational learning'. *Sloan Management Review,* 35, 1, pp. 37–50.

Kirkwood, G and Kirkwood, C (1989) *Living Adult Education: Freire in Scotland.* Edinburgh, Scottish Institute of Adult and Continuing Education/Open University Press.

Knapper, C and Cropley, A (1985) *Lifelong Learning and Higher Education.* London, Kogan Page.

Knowles, M (1970) *The Modern Practice of Adult Education: From Pedagogy to Andragogy.* Cambridge, Cambridge Book Company.

—— (1973) *The Adult Learner: A Neglected Species.* Houston, Gulf Publishing Co.

—— (1985) *Andragogy in Action: Applying Modern Principles of Adult Learning.* San Francisco, Jossey-Bass.

Kolb, D (1984) *Experiential Learning: Experience as the Source of Learning and Development*. Englewood Cliffs, Prentice Hall.

Kolb, D, Lublin, S, Spoth, J and Baker, R (1986) 'Strategic management development: using experiential learning to assess and develop managerial competences'. *Journal of Management Development*, 5, 3, pp. 13–24.

Krajnc, A (1989) 'Andragogy', pp. 19–21 in C Titmus (ed.) *Lifelong Education for Adults: An International Handbook*. Oxford, Pergamon.

Lambert, S (1990) 'Processes linking work and family: a critical review and research agenda'. *Human Relations*, 43, 3, pp. 239–57.

Latack, J (1984) 'Career transitions within organisations: an exploratory study of work, nonwork and coping strategies'. *Organisational Behaviour and Human Performance*, 34, pp. 296–322.

Lawson, K (1974) 'Learning situations or educational situations?, *Adult Education*, 47, pp. 88–92.

—— (1977) *A Critique of Recurrent Education*. Nottingham, Association for Recurrent Education, Discussion Paper No. 1.

—— (1982a) 'Lifelong education: concept or policy?' *International Journal of Lifelong Education*, 1, 2, pp. 97–108.

—— (1982b) *Analysis and Ideology: Conceptual Essays on the Education of Adults*. Nottingham, University of Nottingham Department of Adult Education.

Lawton, D and Gordon, P (1993) *Dictionary of Education*. Sevenoaks, Hodder and Stoughton.

Layard, R, Mayhew, K and Owen, G (eds) (1994) *Britain's Training Deficit*. Aldershot, Avebury.

Lengrand, P (1975) *An Introduction to Lifelong Education*. London, Croom Helm.

—— (1989) 'Lifelong education: growth of the concept', pp. 5–9 in C Titmus (ed.) *Lifelong Education for Adults: An International Handbook*. Oxford, Pergamon.

Lessem, R (1991) *Total Quality Learning: Building a Learning Organization*. Oxford, Blackwell.

—— (1993) *Business as a Learning Community: Applying Global Concepts to Organizational Learning*. Maidenhead, McGraw-Hill.

Levin, H and Schütze, H (1983) 'Economic and political dimensions of recurrent education', pp. 9–36 in H Levin and H Schütze (eds) *Financing Recurrent Education: Strategies for Increasing Employment, Job Opportunities and Productivity*. Beverly Hills, Sage.

Lewis, R (1986) 'What is open learning?'. *Open Learning*, 1, 2, pp. 5–10.

Lewis, R and Spencer, D (1986) *What Is Open Learning?* London, Council for Educational Technology.

Lloyd, C and Cook, A (1993) *Implementing Standards of Competence: Practical Strategies for Industry*. London, Kogan Page.

Long, D (1990) *Learner Managed Learning: The Key to Lifelong Learning and Development*. London, Kogan Page.

Lovett, T (1982) *Adult Education, Community Development and the Working Class*. Nottingham, University of Nottingham Department of Adult Education, second edition.

Lovett, T, Clarke, C and Kilmurray, A (1983) *Adult Education and*

Community Action. London, Croom Helm.

Mabey, C and Iles, P (1994) 'Career development practices in the UK: a participant perspective', pp. 123–32 in C Mabey and P Iles (eds), *Managing Learning*. London, Routledge.

McConnell, C (1982) 'Definitions, methods, paradigms', pp. 1–11 in L Bidwell and C McConnell (eds) *Community Education and Community Development*. Aberdeen, Northern College of Education.

MacDonald, R and Coffield, F (1991) *Risky Business? Youth and the Enterprise Culture*. London, Falmer Press.

McGill, I and Beaty, L (1992) *Action Learning: a Practitioner's Guide*. London, Kogan Page.

McGivney, V (1990) *Education's For Other People: Access to Education for Non-participant Adults*. Leicester, National Institute of Adult Continuing Education.

—— (1992) *Tracking Adult Learning Routes: A Pilot Investigation into Adult Learners' Starting Points and Progression to Further Education and Training*. Leicester, National Institute of Adult Continuing Education.

—— (1993) *Women, Education and Training: Barriers to Access, Informal Starting Points and Progression Routes*. Leicester, National Institute of Adult Continuing Education.

McIlroy, J and Spencer, B (1988) *University Adult Education in Crisis*. Leeds, University of Leeds, Department of Adult and Continuing Education.

MacKenzie, N, Postgate, R and Scupham, J (1975) *Open Learning: Systems and Problems in Post-secondary Education*. Paris, UNESCO.

Mackie, R (ed.) (1980) *Literacy and Revolution: The Pedagogy of Paulo Freire*. London, Pluto Press.

McLaren, P and Lankshear, C (eds) (1994) *Politics of Liberation: Paths from Freire*. London, Routledge.

McNay, I (1988) 'Open learning: a jarring note', pp. 130–9 in N Paine (ed.) *Open Learning in Transition: An Agenda for Action*. Cambridge, National Extension College.

Maguire, M, Maguire, S and Felstead, A (1993) *Factors Influencing Individual Commitment to Lifetime Learning: A Literature Review*. Sheffield, Employment Department.

Marginson, S (1995) 'Markets in higher education: Australia', pp. 17–39 in J Smyth (ed.) *Academic Work*. Buckingham, Open University Press.

Marquardt, M and Reynolds, A (1994) *The Global Learning Organisation*. Burr Ridge, Illinois, Irwin Professional Publishing.

Martin, I (1987) 'Community education: towards a theoretical analysis', pp. 9–32 in G Allen, J Bastiani, I Martin and K Richards (eds) *Community Education: An Agenda for Educational Reform*. Milton Keynes, Open University Press.

Martin, L (1986) *Helping Adults Learn: A Theory of Andragogy*. Sheffield, Association for Recurrent Education.

Marton, F, Hounsell, D and Entwistle, N (eds) (1984) *The Experience of Learning*. Edinburgh, Scottish Academic Press.

Mason, R and Kaye, A (eds) (1989) *Mindweave: Communications, Computers and Distance Education*. Oxford, Pergamon Press.

Matthews, M (1980) 'Knowledge, action and power', pp. 82–92 in R
Mackie (ed.) *Literacy and Revolution: The Pedagogy of Paulo Freire.*
London, Pluto Press.

Mayo, A and Lank, E (1994) *The Power of Learning: A Guide to Gaining
Competitive Advantage.* London, Institute of Personnel and Development.

Megginson, D, Joy-Matthews, J and Banfield, P (1993) *Human Resource
Development.* London, Kogan Page.

Metcalf, H (1993) *Non-Traditional Students' Experience of Higher Education:
A Review of the Literature.* London, Committee of Vice-Chancellors and
Principals.

Mezirow, J (1981) 'A critical theory of adult learning and education'.
Adult Education (USA), 32, 1, pp. 3–24.

Michaels, R (1986) 'Entry routes for mature students: variety and quality
assessed'. *Journal of Access Studies*, 1, 1, pp. 57–71.

Molander, C and Winterton, J (1994) *Managing Human Resources.* London,
Routledge.

Molloy, S and Carroll, V (1992) *Progress and Performance in Higher
Education: A Report on Performance Monitoring of 'Standard' and 'Non-
standard' Entrants to Undergraduate Courses.* London, Council for
National Academic Awards.

Molyneux, F, Low, G and Fowler, G (eds) (1988) *Learning for Life: Politics
and Progress in Recurrent Education.* London, Croom Helm.

Moore, M (1983) 'On a theory of independent study', pp. 68–94 in D
Sewart, D Keegan and B Holmberg (eds) *Distance Education: International Perspectives.* London, Croom Helm.

—— (1990) 'Recent contributions to the theory of distance education'.
Open Learning, 5, 3, pp. 10–15.

Morgan, C and Murgatroyd, S (1994) *Total Quality Management in the
Public Sector: An International Perspective.* Buckingham, Open University Press.

Mulder, M (1990) 'Training and development in organisations: an inter-
national research perspective', pp. 63–83 in M Mulder, A
Romiszowski and P van der Sijde (eds) *Strategic Human Resource
Development.* Amsterdam, Swets and Zeitlinger.

Mumford, A (1991) 'Individual and organisational learning'. *Industrial
and Commercial Training*, 23, 6, pp. 24–31.

Nadler, L and Nadler, Z (eds) (1990) *The Handbook of Human Resource
Development.* New York, John Wiley, second edition.

National Advisory Body for Local Authority Higher Education (1984)
Report of the Continuing Education Working Group. London, NAB.

National Commission on Education (1993) *Learning to Succeed: A Radical
Look at Education Today and a Strategy for the Future.* London,
Heinemann.

National Extension College *(1981) Flexistudy: Some Questions Answered.*
Cambridge, NEC.

National Institute for Adult Continuing Education (1989) *Adults in
Higher Education: A Policy Discussion Paper.* Leicester, NIACE.

—— (1994) *What Price the Learning Society?.* Leicester, NIACE.

Newman, M (1979) *The Poor Cousin: A Study of Adult Education*. London, George Allen and Unwin.

Nicholson, M and West, M (1988) *Managerial Job Change: Men and Women in Transition*. Cambridge, Cambridge University Press.

Nyberg, D (ed.) (1975) *The Philosophy of Open Education*. London, Routledge and Kegan Paul.

Oakeshott, M (1967) 'Learning and teaching', pp. 156–76 in R Peters (ed.) *The Concept of Education*. London, Routledge and Kegan Paul.

Open University (1976) *Report of the Committee on Continuing Education*. Milton Keynes, Open University.

O'Reilly, D (1991) 'Developing opportunities for independent learners'. *Open Learning*, 6, 3, pp. 3–13.

Organization for Economic Cooperation and Development (1973) *Recurrent Education: A Strategy for Lifelong Learning*. Paris, OECD.

—— (1977) *Learning Opportunities for Adults. Volume IV: Participation in Adult Education*. Paris, OECD.

—— (1992) *Education at a Glance: OECD Indicators*. Paris, OECD.

Otala, L (1992) *European Approaches to Lifelong Learning: Trends in Industry Practices and Industry–university Cooperation in Adult Education and Training*. Paris, CRE Action 92.

Oxenham, J (ed.) (1984) *Education Versus Qualifications? A Study of Relationships Between Education, Selection for Employment and Productivity of Labour*. London, George Allen & Unwin.

Parry, G and Wake, C (eds) (1990) *Access and Alternative Futures for Higher Education*. London, Hodder and Stoughton.

Pascarella, E and Terenzini, P (1991) *How College Affects Students: Findings and Insights from Twenty Years of Research*. San Francisco, Jossey-Bass.

Paterson, R (1979) *Values, Education and the Adult*. London, Routledge and Kegan Paul.

Paul, R (1990) *Open Learning and Open Management: Leadership and Integrity in Distance Education*. London, Kogan Page.

Pedler, M, Burgoyne, J and Boydell, T (1991) *The Learning Company: A Strategy for Sustainable Development*. London, McGraw-Hill.

Penland, P (1979) 'Self-initiated learning'. *Adult Education* (USA), 29, 3, pp. 170–9.

Percy, K, Ramsden, P and Lewin, J (1980) *Independent Study: Two Examples from English Higher Education*. Guildford, Society for Research into Higher Education.

Perraton, H (1987) 'Theories, generalisation and practice in distance education'. *Open Learning*, 2, 3, pp. 3–12.

Perry, W (1976) *Open University: A Personal Account by the First Vice-Chancellor*. Milton Keynes, Open University Press.

Peters, O (1983) 'Distance education and industrial production: a comparative interpretation in outline', pp. 95–113 in D Sewart, D Keegan and B Holmberg (eds), *Distance Education: International Perspectives*. Beckenham, Croom Helm.

Peters, R (1966) *Ethics and Education*. London, George Allen and Unwin.

—— (ed.) (1967) *The Concept of Education*. London, Routledge and Kegan Paul.

Peters, T (1987) *Thriving on Chaos*. London, Macmillan.

Phillips, A and Taylor, B (1986) 'Sex and skill', pp. 54–66 in Feminist Review (ed.) *Waged Work: A Reader*. London, Virago.

Plant, R (1974) *Community and Ideology: An Essay in Applied Social Philosophy*. London, Routledge and Kegan Paul.

Pollert, A (ed.) (1991) *Farewell to Flexibility?* Oxford, Blackwell.

Poster, C and Kruger, A (eds) (1990) *Community Education in the Western World*. London, Routledge.

Poster, C and Zimmer, J (eds.) (1992) *Community Education in the Third World*. London, Routledge.

Preston, R (1982) *Theories of Development*. London, Routledge and Kegan Paul.

—— (1985) *New Trends in Development Theory: Essays in Development and Social Theory*. London, Routledge and Kegan Paul.

Pring, R (1993) 'Liberal education and vocational preparation', pp. 49–78 in R Barrow and P White (eds) *Beyond Liberal Education: Essays in Honour of Paul Hirst*. London, Routledge.

Psacharopoulos, G (ed.) (1987) *Economics of Education: Research and Studies*. Oxford, Pergamon.

Raggatt, P (1993) 'Post-Fordism and distance education: a flexible strategy for change'. *Open Learning*, 8, 1, pp. 21–31.

Ram, G (1989) *Going Modular*. London, Council for National Academic Awards.

Ranson, S (1992) 'Towards the learning society'. *Educational Management and Administration*, 20, 2, pp. 68–79.

—— (1994) *Towards the Learning Society*. London, Cassell.

Rees, T (1992) *Women and the Labour Market*. London, Routledge.

Revans, R (1982) *The Origins and Growth of Action Learning*. Lund, Studentlitteratur.

Richardson, J, Eysenck, M and Piper, D (eds) (1987) *Student Learning: Research in Education and Cognitive Psychology*. Milton Keynes, Open University Press.

Rix, A, Parkinson, R and Gaunt, R (1994) *Investors in People: A Qualitative Study of Employers*. Sheffield, Employment Department.

Roberts, D, Higgins, T and Lloyd, R (1992) *Higher Education: The Student Experience*. Leeds, HEIST.

Rogers, A (1986) *Teaching Adults*. Milton Keynes, Open University Press.

Rogers, C et al. (1983) *Freedom to Learn for the 80s*. Columbus, Ohio, Charles Merrill.

Rogers, J (1989) *Adults Learning*. Milton Keynes, Open University Press.

Romiszowski, A (1990) 'Trends in corporate training and development', pp. 17–48 in M Mulder, A Romiszowski and P van der Sijde (eds) *Strategic Human Resource Development*. Amsterdam, Swets and Zeitlinger.

Rubenson, K (1977) *Participation in Recurrent Education: A Research Review*. Paris, Organization for Economic Cooperation and Development.

—— (1987) 'Participation in recurrent education: a research review', pp. 39–67 in H Schütze and D Istance (eds) *Recurrent Education Revisited:*

Modes of Participation and Financing. Stockholm, Almqvist and Wiksell.

Rumble, G (1986) *The Planning and Management of Distance Education*. Beckenham, Croom Helm.

—— (1989) '"Open learning", "distance learning", and the misuse of language'. *Open Learning*, 4, 2, pp. 28–36.

—— (1995) 'Labour market theories and distance education 1: industrialisation and distance education'. *Open Learning*, 10, 1, pp. 10–20.

Rumble, G and Harry, K (eds) (1982) *The Distance Teaching Universities*. Beckenham, Croom Helm.

Sacks, H (1980) 'Flexistudy: an open learning system for further and adult education'. *British Journal of Educational Technology*, 11, 2, pp. 85–95.

Sargant, N (1991) *Learning and Leisure: A Study of Adult Participation in Learning and its Policy Implications*. Leicester, National Institute of Adult Continuing Education.

Schön, D (1971) *Beyond the Stable State: Public and Private Learning in a Changing Society*. London, Temple Smith.

—— (1983) *The Reflective Practitioner: How Professionals Think in Action*. London, Temple Smith.

—— (1988) *Educating the Reflective Practitioner*. San Francisco, Jossey-Bass.

Schultz, T (1961) 'Investment in human capital'. *American Economic Review*, 51, 1, pp. 1–17.

—— (1971) *Investment in Human Capital: The Role of Education and of Research*. New York, Free Press.

Schütze, H and Istance, D (eds) (1987) *Recurrent Education Revisited: Modes of Participation and Financing*. Stockholm, Almqvist and Wiksell.

Scottish Education Department (1982) *Distance No Object: Examples of Open Learning in Scotland*. Edinburgh, HMSO.

—— (1983) *Education in the Community*. Edinburgh, HMSO.

Senge, P (1990) *The Fifth Discipline: The Art and Practice of the Learning Organisation*. New York, Doubleday.

Shale, D (1990) 'Toward a reconceptualisation of distance education', pp. 331–43 in M Moore, P Cookson, J Donaldson and B Quigley (eds) *Contemporary Issues in American Distance Education*. Oxford, Pergamon.

Shale, D and Garrison, D (1990) 'Education and communication', pp. 23–39 in D Garrison and D Shale (eds) *Education at a Distance: From Issues to Practice*. Malabar, Florida, Robert Krieger.

Shuttleworth, D (1993) *Enterprise Learning in Action: Education and Economic Renewal for the Twenty-first Century*. London, Routledge.

Silver, H (1988) *Intentions and Outcomes: Vocationalism in Further Education*. Harlow, Longman/Further Education Unit.

Simosko, S (1991) *Accreditation of Prior Learning: A Practical Guide for Professionals*. London, Kogan Page.

Sinclair, M (1991) 'Women, work and skill: economic theories and feminist perspectives', pp. 1–24 in M Redclift and M Sinclair (eds), *Working Women: International Perspectives on Labour and Gender Ideology*. London, Routledge.

Sloboda, J (1986) 'What is skill?', pp. 16–25 in A Gellatly (ed.) *The Skilful Mind: An Introduction to Cognitive Psychology*. Milton Keynes, Open University Press.

Smith, D, Macaulay, J and Associates (1980) *Participation in Social and Political Activities*. San Francisco, Jossey-Bass.

Smith, P and Kelly, M (eds.) (1987) *Distance Education and the Mainstream: Convergence in Education*. London, Croom Helm.

Smith, R (1983) *Learning How to Learn: Applied Theory for Adults*. Milton Keynes, Open University Press.

Smithers, A and Griffin, A (1986) *The Progress of Mature Students*. Manchester, Joint Matriculation Board.

Smithers, A, and Robinson, P (1989) *Increasing Participation in Higher Education*. London, BP Educational Services.

Sonnenfeld, J and Kotter, J (1982) 'The maturation of career theory'. *Human Relations*, 35, 1, pp. 19–46.

Spencer, L and Taylor, S (1994) *Participation and Progress in the Labour Market: Key Issues for Women*. Sheffield, Employment Department.

Squires, G (1986) *Modularisation*. Manchester, CONTACT.

—— (1987) *The Curriculum Beyond School*. London, Hodder and Stoughton.

—— (1990) *First Degree: the Undergraduate Curriculum*. Milton Keynes, Open University Press.

Stephenson, J (1980) 'Higher education: school for independent study', pp. 132–49 in T Burgess and E Adams (eds) *Outcomes of Education*. London, Macmillan.

—— (1992) 'Capability and quality in higher education', pp. 1–9 in J Stephenson and S Weil (eds) *Quality in Learning: A Capability Approach in Higher Education*. London, Kogan Page.

Stephenson, J and Weil, S (1992) 'Four themes in educating for capability', pp. 10–18 in J Stephenson and S Weil (eds) *Quality in Learning: A Capability Approach in Higher Education*. London, Kogan Page.

Super, D (1980) 'A life-span, life-space approach to career development'. *Journal of Vocational Behaviour*, 16, pp. 282–98.

Tait, A (ed.) (1993) *Key Issues in Open Learning: A Reader. An Anthology from the Journal 'Open Learning', 1986–1992*. Harlow, Longman.

Tarsh, J (1989) 'New graduate destinations by age on graduation'. *Employment Gazette*, 97, pp. 581–98.

Tasker, M and Packham, D (1994) 'Changing cultures? Government intervention in higher education 1987–93'. *British Journal of Educational Studies*, 42, 2, pp. 150–62.

Taylor, P (1993) *The Texts of Paulo Freire*. Buckingham, Open University Press.

Tennant, M (1988) *Psychology and Adult Learning*. London, Routledge.

Theodossin, E (1986) *In Search of the Responsive College*. Bristol, Further Education Staff College.

Thirlwall, A (1994) *Growth and Development: With Special Reference to Developing Economies*. London, Macmillan, fifth edition.

Thomas, A (1991) *Beyond Education: A New Perspective on Society's Management of Learning*. San Francisco, Jossey-Bass.

Thomas, D (ed.) (1995) *Flexible Learning Strategies in Higher and Further Education*. London, Cassell.

Thomas, J (1982) *Radical Adult Education: Theory and Practice*. Nottingham, University of Nottingham, Department of Adult Education.

Thomas, L and Harri-Augstein, S (1985) *Self-organised Learning: Foundations of a Conversational Science for Psychology*. London, Routledge and Kegan Paul.

Thomson, R and Mabey, C (1994) *Developing Human Resources*. Oxford, Butterworth-Heinemann.

Thorpe, M and Grugeon, D (eds) (1987) *Open Learning for Adults*. Harlow, Longman.

Tight, M (ed.) (1983) *Adult Learning and Education*. London, Croom Helm.

—— (1987) 'Mixing distance and face-to-face higher education'. *Open Learning*, 2, 1, pp. 14–18.

—— (1989) 'The ideology of higher education', pp. 85–98 in O Fulton (ed.) *Access and Institutional Change*. Milton Keynes, Open University Press.

—— (1993) 'Access, not access courses: maintaining a broad vision', pp. 62–74 in R Edwards, S Sieminski, and D Zeldin (eds) *Adult Learners, Education and Training*. London, Routledge.

—— (1994) 'Utopia and the education of adults'. *International Journal of University Adult Education*, 33, 2, pp. 29–44.

—— (1995) 'Education, work and adult life: a literature review'. *Research Papers in Education*, 10, 3, pp. 381–98.

Tinto, V (1987) *Leaving College: Rethinking the Causes and Cures of Student Attrition*. Chicago, University of Chicago Press.

Titmus, C (ed.) (1989) *Lifelong Education for Adults: An International Handbook*. Oxford, Pergamon.

Toffler, A (1970) *Future Shock*. London, Bodley Head.

—— (1980) *The Third Wave*. London, Collins.

Tomlinson, P and Kilner, S (1990) *Flexible Learning, Flexible Teaching: The Flexible Learning Framework and Current Educational Theory*. Leeds, University of Leeds School of Education.

Tough, A (1971) *The Adult's Learning Projects: A Fresh Approach to Theory and Practice in Adult Learning*. Toronto, Ontario Institute for Studies in Education.

—— (1976) 'Self-directed learning and major personal change', pp. 57–75 in R Smith (ed.) *Adult Learning: Issues and Innovations*. ERIC Clearinghouse in Career Education.

—— (1989) 'Self-directed learning: concepts and practice', pp. 256–60 in C Titmus (ed.) *Lifelong Education for Adults: An International Handbook*. Oxford, Pergamon.

Tovey, P (1994) *Quality Assurance in Continuing Professional Education: An Analysis*. London, Routledge.

Training Agency (1989) *Training in Britain: A Study of Funding, Activity and Attitudes*. London, HMSO, five volumes.

—— (1989) *Enterprise in Higher Education: Key Features of the Proposals 1988–89*. Sheffield, Training Agency.

—— (1990) *Enterprise in Higher Education: Key Features of the Proposals 1989–90*. Sheffield, Training Agency.

Tuijnman, A (1989) *Recurrent Education, Earnings and Well-being: A Fifty Year Longitudinal Study of a Cohort of Swedish Men*. Stockholm, Almqvist & Wiksell.

Unit for the Development of Adult Continuing Education (1989) *Understanding Competence: A Development Paper*. Leicester, UDACE.

United Nations Educational, Scientific and Cultural Organisation (1989) *Statistical Yearbook 1989*. Paris, UNESCO.

University Grants Committee (1984) *Report of the Continuing Education Working Party*. London, UGC.

Usher, R and Edwards, R (1994) *Postmodernism and Education*. London, Routledge.

Verduin, J and Clark, T (1991) *Distance Education: The Foundations of Effective Practice*. San Francisco, Jossey-Bass.

Vroeijenstijn, A (1995) *Improvement and Accountability: Navigating between Scylla and Charybdis. Guide for External Quality Assessment in Higher Education*. London, Jessica Kingsley.

Wade, W, Hodgkinson, K, Smith, A and Arfield, J (eds) (1994) *Flexible Learning in Higher Education*. London, Kogan Page.

Wain, K (1987) *Philosophy of Lifelong Education*. London, Croom Helm.

—— (1993) 'Lifelong education and adult education: the state of the theory'. *International Journal of Lifelong Education*, 12, 2, pp. 86–99.

Walker, L (1994) 'The new higher education systems, modularity and student capability', pp. 24–42 in A Jenkins and L Walker (eds) *Developing Student Capability Through Modular Courses*. London, Kogan Page.

Ward, K and Taylor, R (eds) (1986) *Adult Education and the Working Class: Education for the Missing Millions*. London, Croom Helm.

Watkins, K (1991) 'Many voices: defining human resource development from different disciplines'. *Adult Education Quarterly*, 41, 4, pp. 241–55.

Watkins, K and Marsick, V (1992) 'Building the learning organisation: a new role for human resource developers'. *Studies in Continuing Education*, 14, 2, pp. 115–29.

Watson, D, Brooks, J, Coghill, C, Lindsay, R and Scurry, D (1989) *Managing the Modular Course: Perspectives from Oxford Polytechnic*. Milton Keynes, Open University Press.

Watts, A (1981) 'Career patterns', pp. 213–45 in A Watts, D Super and J Kidd (eds) *Career Development in Britain: Some Contributions to Theory and Practice*. Cambridge, Hobsons Press.

Wedemeyer, C (1981) *Learning at the Back Door: Reflections on Non-traditional Learning in the Lifespan*. Madison, University of Wisconsin Press.

Weil, S (1986) 'Non-traditional learners within traditional higher education institutions: discovery and disappointment'. *Studies in Higher Education*, 11, 3, pp. 219–35.

Weil, S and McGill, I (eds.) (1989) *Making Sense of Experiential Learning: Diversity in Theory and Practice*. Milton Keynes, Open University Press.

Welsh, L and Woodward, P (1989) *Continuing Professional Development: Towards a National Strategy*. London, Further Education Unit.

White, B, Cox, C and Cooper, C (1992) *Women's Career Development: A Study of High Flyers*. Oxford, Blackwell.

Williams, G (1977) *Towards Lifelong Education: A New Role for Higher Education Institutions*. Paris, UNESCO.

Williams, K (1994) 'Vocationalism and liberal education: exploring the tensions'. *Journal of the Philosophy of Education*, 28, 1, pp. 89–100.

Williams, R (1988) *Keywords: A Vocabulary of Culture and Society*. London, Fontana, first edition 1976.

Wiltshire, H (1956) 'The great tradition in university adult education'. *Adult Education*, 29, 2, pp. 88–97.

Wolf, A (1995) *Competence-based Assessment*. Buckingham, Open University Press.

Woodhall, M (1987) 'Human capital concepts', pp. 21–4 in G Psacharo-poulos (ed.) *Economics of Education: Research and Studies*. Oxford, Pergamon.

Woodley, A and Parlett, M (1983) 'Student drop-out'. *Teaching at a Distance*, 24, pp. 2–23.

Woodley, A, Wagner, L, Slowey, M, Hamilton, M and Fulton, O (1987) *Choosing to Learn: Adults in Education*. Milton Keynes, Open University Press.

Working Group on Vocational Qualifications (1986) *Review of Vocational Qualifications in England and Wales*. London, HMSO.

Wright, P (1991) 'Access or accessibility'. *Journal of Access Studies*, 6, 1, pp. 6–15.

Young, M (ed.) (1971) *Knowledge and Control: New Directions for the Sociology of Education*. London, Collier Macmillan.

Zuber-Skerritt, O and Ryan, Y (eds) (1994) *Quality in Postgraduate Education*. London, Kogan Page.

Index